Adiós Chimayó bonito
Adiós puertas encaladas
Adiós muchachas bonitas
Adiós viejitas arrugadas.

(An old Chimayó verso)

Benigna's Chimayó

Cuentos from the Old Plaza

By Don J. Usner

As Told by Benigna Ortega Chávez

Translations by Stella Chávez Usner and Carole Usner-Hunt
With Illustrations by Arturo Antonio Usner y Chávez
and Photographs by Don J. Usner

Museum of New Mexico Press   Santa Fe

*For my father, Arthur Anthony Usner, who fell in love with my mother
and Chimayó at first sight and decided to make his home in New Mexico; and for
my mother, Stella Chávez Usner, whose strength, patience, and love never cease
to inspire me.*

Project editor: Mary Wachs
Design and production: David Skolkin
Composition: Set in New Caledonia with Post Antiqua display.
Manufactured in Korea
10 9 8 7 6 5 4 3 2 1

Library of Congress Cataloging-in-Publication Data
Usner, Donald J.
Benigna's Chimayó : Cuentos from the Old Plaza / by Don J. Usner;
as told by Benigna Ortega Chávez;
translations by Stella Chávez Usner and
Carole Usner-Hunt; with illustrations by Arturo Antonio Usner y Chávez.
p. cm.
ISBN 0-89013-381-6 (cloth)—ISBN 0-89013-382-4 (pbk.)
1. Tales-New Mexico-Chimayó. 2. Hispanic American-New
Mexico-Chimayó-Folklore. I. Chávez, Benigna Ortega. II. Title.
GR110.N6 U75 2001
398.2'089'680789-DC21   00-048972

MUSEUM OF NEW MEXICO PRESS
Post Office Box 2087
Santa Fe, New Mexico 87504

Cover photograph: Benigna Ortega Chávez, ca. 1989. Photo by Don J. Usner
Photograph on page ii: Don Usner with his grandmother, Benigna Ortega Chávez, 1992. Photo by Don J. Usner
Back cover: Plaza del Cerro, Chimayó, 1995. Photo by Don. J. Usner

Contents

Acknowledgments

OF THEIR FOUR HUNDRED YEARS IN THE NEW WORLD, we know only that these cuentos came to Chimayó and into the twentieth century through eight generations of the Ortega family. Thanks to Grabiel Ortega and Ana Bartola López; Manuel Ortega and Ana María Gonzales; Gervacio Ortega and Guadalupe Vigil; José Ramón Ortega and Petra Maestas; and Reyes Ortega and Genoveva Quintana. Reyes's sister, Bonefacia, and perhaps others in the extended family also helped pass the stories along. These people took the time to tell the cuentos to children through five generations and thereby gave them safe passage from the eighteenth into the twentieth century.

Of course, greatest thanks go to the cuentos-bearers of the sixth and seventh generations in the family lineage: my grandma, Benigna Ortega Chávez, and my mother, Stella Chávez Usner. These remarkable women lovingly passed the cuentos to my siblings and me. My mother also deserves full credit for recording the stories on paper and giving me full access to her transcriptions. She also played an active role in shaping my rewrites by patiently going over each word and offering suggestions and corrections.

I'm also indebted to my sister, Carole Usner-Hunt, for her tireless work on the Spanish translations of the cuentos as I rewrote them. This proved to be a much more daunting task than we had anticipated, especially as Carole strove to retain the flavor of the regional dialect, often against the dictums of her training in contemporary Spanish.

The drawings that my brother, Arturo Antonio Usner y Chávez, produced for this collection brought it to a new level of expression. The evocative artwork reveals his own vivid memories of the cuentos and portray the characters precisely as Grandma described them.

Enrique la Madrid has tracked this project for years through many phases of planning and execution. His initial push of inspiration and advice persisted through to the book's conclusion, and his reading of the final Spanish translations proved invaluable.

In the final hour, and on short notice, Jim Gavin also helped with the task of balancing the idiom of the *la gente norteña* with modern Spanish.

The Lannan Foundation of Santa Fe—and particularly my friend and mentor there, Janet Voorhees—has been tremendously supportive in many ways, not the least of which was the grant of a month-long residency at a writing retreat where I produced the final draft of the book.

Mary Wachs again served me in multitudinous ways that the nominal title of editor fails to adequately describe. She had the vision to support the idea for this project from its inception and also maintained the patience to remain consistently positive on the way to completing the book.

My sisters Ellen Leitner and Janice Wills encouraged me throughout the writing process and also remembered occasional details and additions to the stories, which I included. Thanks also to William deBuys, who proved a good friend and solid supporter in many ways and who also read portions of the final manuscript; and to numerous friends and relatives in Chimayó who prodded me along, including my tía Melita Ortega, Peter Malmgren, Lucy Collier, Andrew Ortega, Eleanor Martinez, Chris and Ruth Brown, Raymond Bal, Mely Muñoz, and Esperanza Vigil.

My daughter, Jennifer, brought enough joy to keep a flotilla afloat through the completion of the manuscript. And underpinning the whole operation, my wife, Deborah, has proved herself more resilient than I imagined a person could be.

Translator's Note

MY MOTHER, STELLA CHÁVEZ USNER, and my grandma, Benigna Ortega Chávez, speak the New Mexico dialect of Spanish, which is characterized by many unique features such as words surviving from the sixteenth and seventeeth centuries (called archaisms); words borrowed from Nahuatl, the language of the Aztecs; and words adapted from English. The dialect is considered to be nonstandard in the preservation of these words as well as in its departure from standard Spanish in certain grammatical and linguistic aspects. In translating these stories, Stella, Don, and I decided to preserve these elements in spite of the fact that they are considered to be nonstandard. In deciding this, we stay true to the authenticity of the dialect as spoken by my grandma and pay tribute to all speakers of the dialect. Rather than regarding the translation as inaccurate or incorrect, I hope that the Spanish reader will keep an open mind and enjoy the beauty of the dialect.

Some examples of words found in the stories from the dialect are as follows:

NEW MEXICO	STANDARD EQUIVALENT	TRANSLATION
vido (archaism)	vio	he/she saw
vía (archaism)	veía	used to see/was seeing
truje (archaism)	traje	I brought
trujieron (archaism)	trajeron	they brought
traiba (archaism)	traía	he/she used to bring/was bringing
dijieron (linguistic variation)	dijeron	they said
ansina (archaism)	así	so, thus
nadien (archaism)	nadie	no one
tomates, hablates, hicites (archaisms)	tomaste, hablaste, hiciste	you took, you spoke, you did
muncho (archaism)	mucho	much, many, a lot
nojar (linguistic variation)	enojar	to get mad
horcar (linguistic variation)	ahorcar	to hang

NEW MEXICO	STANDARD EQUIVALENT	TRANSLATION
trompezó (linguistic variation)	tropezó	he/she tripped
jito, a (linguistic variation)	hijito	son, daughter (endearing)
rasposo (archaism)	áspero	rough
ha visto (gramatical variation	he visto	I have seen
el hambre (gender change)	el hambre	hunger
recordar (archaism)	despertarse	to wake up
en tal de que (archaism)	con tal de que	provided that
ratones voladores (regional adaptation)	murciélagos	bats
petaquilla	baúl	chest

Benigna's Chimayó

Cuentos from the Old Plaza

Introduction

I WAS BLESSED WITH OPPORTUNITIES to spend time in my youth in Chimayó with my grandmother, Benigna Ortega Chávez. Like all her grandchildren, I took a turn staying with her for a week or two each summer, beginning when I was perhaps five years old and continuing into my teens. During high school years in the early 1970s, my summer visits continued, as I lived with Grandma and wove blankets at the Ortegas' shop across the road. She told me these *cuentos*, or folk stories, during those summer sojourns and later when I came to Chimayó to live as an adult.

Grandma, now 102 years old, tells me that she committed the cuentos to memory as a child when her father, José de los Reyes Ortega, and her aunt, María Bonefacia Ortega, told them to her. *"Muy pronto los aprendí!"* she says. "I learned them so fast. I had a very good memory—even the mission teachers said so—and some of those stories I heard only once, and I remember them still. Now, it's all leaving me, but back then I remembered everything."

Grandma heard these cuentos from her Chimayó elders at bedtime, around the *fogones* in the winter evenings, in the *dispensas* as people gathered to tie chile *ristras*. Though she may have memorized them quickly, she had countless opportunities to pick up new details and stories because in those days "people liked to talk and listen to each other," as she says. Time moved slowly, and there were few distractions to break up the long workdays and nights. But storytelling served as more than entertainment. This is how families heard the latest news, how they passed on family history, and how the young people learned from the *viejitos*. The cuentos formed one part of a rich oral tradition that included *dichos, versos, adivinanzas, trabalenguas, oraciones, canciones*—and just plain old gossip. Grandma recalls examples of all of these almost daily.

Grandma's turn to tell the cuentos came when her mother, Genoveva, died in childbirth, leaving four younger sisters and an infant brother (who died a few months later) in Grandma's care. Grandma was twenty-one and the year was 1919. Less than a year before, the family had endured the death of the eldest daughter, Sabinita, Grandma's only older sibling, who succumbed to the great epidemic of "Spanish" influenza before she reached her twentieth year.

13

Thus Grandma's long tenure as caregiver and storyteller—a role that now has touched four generations of her descendants—began amid tragedy. She settled into caring for her sisters, and it fell to her to tell the bedtime stories that so recently had been recounted by her father. In another few years, Grandma had children of her own to put to bed at night, and the tales provided the nighttime entertainment once again. When my mother began to have children, Grandma pulled the stories from her memory for her *coyotitos*.

The cuentos passed from generation to generation like that—handed down in times of plenty and times of adversity so that they became intertwined with the stories of the people who told them. No doubt countless tragedies and joys marked the dozen or so generations that had passed since the stories arrived from Spain to the New World. Yet by the time of Grandma's youth, the number of tellers in Chimayó was already dwindling: in her father's generation, only Reyes himself and two of his sisters, Bonefacia and Francesquita, spun these curious tales from the Old World, and they told the stories less and less as the twentieth century advanced. Of all Reyes's daughters, only Grandma recounted the stories. In fact, she was the only one among the numerous cousins of her generation to keep them from disappearing altogether.

Those were changing times, and the folklore that had entertained generations of young Chimayosos was beginning to fade in importance. Families were busy adapting to the new cash economy that, along with the Anglo-Americans, had taken over the territory in the late 1800s. Whereas a simple agrarian existence had sustained the people of the valley for more than two hundred years, by the turn of the century the distant drum of industrialization had begun to accelerate the pace of life. Reyes and his siblings responded by innovating and adapting.

Grandma's father started a weaving business near the plaza in the early 1900s, and Tío Nicasio was soon to follow. Tío Rumaldo took up the old family art of weaving also, but, like many other Chimayosos, he joined an exodus of young men who left for the mining districts of Colorado when he needed the cash, returning to Chimayó more tired and haggard each time. Meanwhile, Reyes's sisters—except for the spinster Bonefacia, who stayed at home with her parents—moved away from the plaza to join their spouses and start families of their own.

These social and economic transitions weren't conducive to passing on the cuentos. Men were away for long periods of time, doubling the workload for women back home, and the labor shifted from communal, agrarian tasks employing extended family to a corporate-centered mode focused on profit. Perhaps only Grandma passed on the cuentos because she was among the eldest of her generation and she, more than the others, remembered the old rhythms of life. Or maybe she told the tales simply because she was a natural storyteller.

Whatever her reasons, Grandma carried the tales intact through some of the most jarring periods of transformation that New Mexicans have faced since coming to the New World. Besides the transition to a new economy and a rapid influx of land-hungry settlers from the eastern United States, Grandma witnessed two world wars and turbulent postwar eras, the Great Depression, the tumult of the 1960s and the agony of Vietnam, the launch of the Space Age, and the explosion of microelectronics—not to mention the

Plaza del Cerro, Chimayó, 1995.

deaths of her husband, her two sons, and numerous family members. She has survived these staggering shifts in the cultural milieu and still moves with the pace of that distant era when people took time to sit around the kerosene lamp or corner fireplace listening to *viejitos*.

Much has been swept away in the rush of the past one hundred years. For Grandma, the way people live today is nonsensical. "Everything has changed so much," she laments on the telephone to her octogenarian and nonagenarian friends and relatives. "God doesn't keep the world like he used to. Everything is topsy-turvy, and time isn't the same anymore. It used to be that people worked at certain hours and at others they rested and visited. Now I don't understand what's wrong with people!"

My earliest memories of Grandma form a sketch of her standing in her screened porch, waving good-bye after a family visit. With every departure, I felt sharp pangs of regret leaving her there in her house, which seemed so lonely and small against the towering, rocky hills. I eagerly returned to keep her company, and before long I was her *consenti-do*, her special grandchild. I think all her *nietos* felt that way, and she spoiled us as only a grandmother can. We had complete freedom in Chimayó, once the chores were done, and she fed us like kings with the old-time foods and fresh produce that her neighbors in the valley still grew.

For Grandma, the summer visits gave her a chance to nurture children and tell stories about her life. I never tired of listening to her recollections or to the cuentos, which seemed to fit perfectly into the world of old buildings, laboring farmers, and the magical landscape of Chimayó, even though they came from another place and time. As she told the story "Juan Tonto," I envisioned the young Juan carrying Grandma's own front door on his back as he chased after his mother down the dusty road. The Enchanted Garden in "El Caballero de la Pluma" surely must have been the cottonwood *bosque* along the Ortega ditch, and Grandma's descriptions of "La Tierra de Mogolló" seemed to correspond exactly to the dusty badlands across the arroyo.

I imagined local landscapes, but Spanish colonists brought these tales over from the Old World, through Mexico, and up the torturous trail from Chihuahua to Santa Fe and then to Chimayó. They are filled with medieval images of princesses and castles and kings, and some speak darkly of Spain's Old World enemies, *los moros*. Packed safely in sure memories and passed by word of mouth, the cuentos traveled like burrs tangled in the wool of churro sheep to be transplanted, along with other accoutrements of Iberian culture, at the raw northern frontier of New Spain. And here they took root, to be transmitted in an unbroken chain from the first storyteller to Grandma, who was born here exactly three hundred years after the first European settlers arrived in 1598 to establish homes in the Kingdom of New Mexico.

Grandma's cuentos became as much a part of the grandchildren's summer experiences of Chimayó as were walks in the hills. While they entertained us as much as the Warner Brothers cartoons that greeted us in the mornings, they also subtly conveyed a set of morals, ideals, and values. In his book *The Uses of Enchantment*, Bruno Bettelheim brilliantly describes the manifold ways that folktales facilitate a child's emotional and psychological development, and the cuentos certainly did this for me and my siblings. They provided both the imagery and guidance for navigating the treacherous waters of our nascent unconscious worlds. At the time I couldn't have articulated all that the cuentos instilled in me, but I see now that they led me to believe in magic, faith, and the ultimate vindication of all that is good. Above all, they filled me with wonder and laughter.

Almost all of Grandma's cuentos also communicate the notion that a poor and inexperienced person can find his way to wealth and happiness. Like folktales the world over, most of these stories speak of a dream of attaining riches beyond measure and of living "happily ever after" with a beautiful loved one. This is the perpetual dream of the common person working the land. As in medieval Europe, only the royalty of these tales enjoy material wealth, but the cuentos hold out the hope that some fortunate and honest individuals might gain access to riches through extraordinary wit or with divine or supernatural assistance.

At the same time, some of the stories, such as "Pascual Ranchero," show that wealth and a bookish education are not necessary for happiness. Simple people often prove to be the most capable at understanding life's complexities. In fact, poor people may be spared the complications that accompany wealth and success.

In many ways, the world of late-nineteenth- and early-twentieth-century Northern

New Mexico was not so different from the medieval world in which the cuentos originated. In both, wealth was concentrated in the hands of a few, and more often than not, these few were less than kind to the many in their employ. It was a hardscrabble existence that the New Mexico villagers led. Money was scarce and material possessions few. Winning the favor of "the kings"—which in early-twentieth-century New Mexico could have been any of a number of sheep patrons, landholders, or industrialists—offered the only way out of grinding poverty. From Chimayó, young men traveled far to toil in the mines, on the railroads, on commercial farms—wherever those with capital had created a place for cheap labor.

In the repeated tales of young men facing starvation and "going off to work for the king," we can feel chilling parallels to the difficulties faced by my grandfather Reyes's generation that left home for wage labor in Colorado and Utah. That people told their children stories of the poor managing to succeed in a hostile, alien world is not surprising, for this was the world these children would face as adults. It is also easy to see the cuentos as comforting explanations to youngsters for why their fathers were away for so long.

Barrancas to the east of Chimayó, 1995

Grandma heard the stories once and never forgot them, and my mother, Stella Chávez Usner, also learned them by heart as she grew up. Although my mother usually left it to Grandma to tell the stories to the grandchildren, she nevertheless played a crucial role in perpetuating them. As we reached adulthood, she saw that even though we had heard the cuentos many times, we were unable to recall the various plots and characters at will. Our memories couldn't preserve the stories the way they had been in the past, so Mother interviewed Grandma and patiently recorded them both in Spanish and in English.

Yet when I read the cuentos as Mother transcribed them, I recognized that a literal record of the stories themselves did not convey their fullness. The cool adobe walls and the silence of the bedroom where we heard them were missing, as was the magic of those late summer evenings that seemed to interact with the stories in an alchemy of sensations to become part of the set where the cuentos took place.

The written word also leaves out the work of the storyteller, and Grandma was a master of this art. She never told a story the same way twice; each one was a spontaneous re-creation. With a sudden whim, she would digress, embellish, pause to make a point. She cared about telling the stories just right, and her style stimulated my imagination to fill in vivid detail.

Now has come my time to pass on the cuentos, and I want to convey not only their content but something of their historical context as well as Grandma's language and style of telling. To do this I have rewritten my mother's transcriptions, putting in bits and pieces of stories that I remembered from my youth and adding descriptions of scenes where I may have heard the stories. I've tried to present the story of the stories and to show how together they represent important fibers of a rich cultural tradition that is quickly transforming and losing much of its unique character.

During the rewriting of the cuentos, I turned to my mother and grandmother for feedback and suggestions to ensure that I stayed true to the original story lines. In a strange twist of fate, I found myself telling Grandma the cuentos in the same bedroom where she had told them to me more than thirty years ago. I read the stories to Grandma and she laughed, surprised at the story lines she once knew so well. Sometimes she interrupted to correct me or to add a phrase. Together, we recited the favorite lines and laughed together out loud as we remembered not just the cuento but the whole story of her telling it to me when I was a young boy—the whole story of our times together. For us, the cuentos convey subtle complexes of feeling that reaffirm our bond. Perhaps they've always done that for families.

When I was young, Grandma told the stories in English, her second language but one she knew as well as her native Spanish. Still, she sometimes lapsed into Spanish or abandoned English altogether for short rhyming sections or when a particular expression defied translation. I have left these phrases in my English versions.

As I grew older and began to understand Spanish better, Grandma recounted the stories entirely in her native tongue. I came to realize that the cuentos flow more smoothly in the original language, and that the rhymes and rhythms of that naturally metered parlance do something that cannot be translated. Accordingly, I decided to include Spanish versions here using Grandma's own way of speaking, which represents the peculiar Northern New Mexico dialect filled with archaisms. I called upon my mother and my younger sister, Carole, to help me translate my revisions of the stories into Spanish and to keep the original tone of Grandma's dialect intact. This proved to be an arduous task that demanded much care and devotion.

Most of the Old World conventions brought to Northern New Mexico have disappeared over time, but some ideas and customs still betray their European origins. The cuentos represent one such fragment of the European cloth from which New Mexicans were cut—a remnant that has been interlaced with parts of other cultures of Native America and Europe over the past four hundred years but nonetheless retains the flavor of ancient times and places. The storytellers of Chimayó took remarkable care of the cuentos so that they arrived in the twentieth century relatively intact even as they changed with each telling from the first versions told.

At the same time, because of their ancient roots, there are things about these stories that may strike people today as archaic or unrefined. Family members have debated much about how much they should be edited to make them more acceptable to a modern audience. Much of the delight of the stories comes from some of their indelicate touches, however, and as children we often found these parts to be the most humorous. Consequently, I have chosen to retell them in their entirety, with all the details I remember, and offer only slight modifications.

Every generation has left its mark on these cuentos, for to remain vibrant and accessible for new generations they must change. Like the storytellers before me, I've made my presentation of these cuentos true to Grandma's delivery but have added my own interpretations and colored them with my memories where I felt it appropriate. I hope that this retelling will seed the cuentos into the next century securely, where they can be retold again and again.

Pascual Ranchero

A long, narrow adobe building stands next door to Grandma's house, only a dozen yards away. We always have called it the dispensa, *and the other small outbuilding near her home is the* dispensita—*words that have no literal meaning for me as a child. I regard them as proper names of these curious old structures of my Chimayó universe. Only many years later do I come to understand that* dispensa *means "supply room," dispensary. As a child, the word designates a place of much more significance.*

Both buildings were constructed long before my time, and the dispensa *was already there when Grandma was born, erected by her father to store crops and to house his weaving looms. Grandma takes me into the* dispensita *once in a while on some errand, but we visit the* dispensa *rarely, and it remains more mysterious. It's not hard to pry loose the ancient, tiny padlock and open the handmade door, and I do so one day just to see what's inside. But something makes me hesitate at the threshold. In the heavy, quiet silence I can almost hear the building breathing in hoarse, dusty sighs.*

Puffs of dry dirt rise from the packed mud floor in the main room as I walk in the dispensa. *A single window on the south side lets in a flood of hot-white sunshine that blinds me and leaves the rest of the room darkened. I can see the straw in the floor's surface and the broad strokes where women smoothed the final coat with sheepskins many, many years ago. For a doorstop, there is a single iron leg from a woodstove. I have to prop this against the door to keep it from shutting behind me, enclosing me suddenly and frightfully in the darkness.*

It smells of the old days in here, a smell of earth, wool, and chile. The chile smell comes from the attic, where Reyes, whom I always refer to as my mother and grand-mother do, as Grandpa Reyes or Papa Reyes, stored sacks of chile that remained there after he died. The peppers disintegrated into dust that filtered through every crack in the ceiling latillas. If I breathe in this chile dust too deeply, I'll sneeze, so walking gently and trying not to disturb the dust become a habit in the dispensa.

The smell of wool emanates from the back room, where Grandpa Reyes's weaving looms stand just where he left them the morning he died in 1944. They lean crookedly in the shadows, made of a collection of hand-hewn boards and scavenged lumber held together by wooden pins. It's hard to imagine anyone being able to weave a straight piece on these looms, but Reyes and later Grandma and Grandpa Abedón wove many hundreds of fine blankets on them, the tools of their trade.

This back room has a spare, sacrosanct aura. Besides the looms, its contents include only a wooden cross with Reyes's name and birth and death dates scrawled on it and a small woodstove in the corner that has been there since Reyes's time. The cross—a temporary grave marker until a stone was placed in the cemetery—seems a fitting reminder that this quiet, meditative work space is Reyes's true last resting place.

The middle room is a far cry from Reyes's sanctuary. Here, everything too old to be of use but too valued to be cast away has ended up. Lying about are rusting oil-burning and gas heaters, several bed frames, bedsprings and mattresses (handmade by Grandma and stuffed with wool from Reyes's sheep), worn enameled buckets, brooms made of wild grass, sections of stovepipe, boxes of plumbing parts, and a crate full of homemade lye soap that Grandma still uses on us occasionally, causing an unforgettable skin burn. Grandpa Reyes's overalls—the very ones I've seen in old photos of him standing at his looms—lie neatly folded in a wooden box, his handkerchiefs tucked into their pockets. There's a crate that once held wool, with the shipping label intact: From Clasgens Yarns in Ohio to Reyes Ortega in Española. Alongside all the castoffs, toys from yesteryear—a wooden Radio Flyer wagon; a tiny, pedal-powered Caterpillar tractor; a wooden rocking horse—seem so well cared for that they could still be used, but I'm not allowed.

In one corner, the last remnants of Reyes's hand tools are stacked, tools Grandma still uses. There's an ax with a head so worn that it doesn't chop wood so much as crush it, a shovel whose blade is ground down to less than half its normal size, and a hoe in a similar state. A scythe and a rake, a handsaw, a pickax. Looking at the wear on each tool, you can feel the ache in Reyes's back.

The mud walls in the dispensa were smoothed to a fine finish and then painted waist-high with the old kind of yeso made from baked and crushed gypsum rock. Even though there are nicks and holes in the yeso where the underlying mud shows through, the white wainscoting gives the dispensa a kind of refinement—an elegance heightened by the carefully painted white wood trim around the windows. Above the *white wall, the smooth, dark brown plaster continues up to the* vigas, *still intact and marked with the knife strokes from the day they were peeled. Two simple wooden sconces—hand cut from rough wood, like the looms—hold up kerosene lamps filled with fuel and waiting for Reyes's match.*

I'm staring at the crate of lye soap and plotting ways to destroy it when suddenly I hear Grandma's voice behind me, crying, "Donnie, Donnie! Where are you, a dónde andas?" *I jump from my reverie to see her coming through the low door, a black silhouette against the noonday sun.* "I've been looking for you all over, 'jito. Come help me wring out the laundry. Didn't you know I was washing?"

She looks around in the dispensa *and abruptly forgets her chores, as if she perceives what I've been seeing, and finds herself absorbed in memories.*

"Ay, cómo me acuerdo yo de este cuarto," *she says.* "My father used to weave in there by kerosene light on winter nights. We'd come over to see him laying down row after row of wool. He worked so hard, bent over that loom—and for what? He's gone now, and all those hundreds of blankets he wove, where are they?*

"I remember when Papa was putting mud on the roof of this house, before the tin roof was on top. He was up there spreading the mud and straw, and we had a ladder and we were bringing him mud in buckets, Petrita and I. And we used to come here in the fall to tie chiles into* ristras *and shuck corn, too. That was work, I'll tell you, en esos días, oh cómo trabajábanos. We tied until our fingers ached, with just a kerosene lamp to see by, and then in the morning, it was off to the* huerta *again to pick chiles.*

"But we had fun, you know. We laughed and told riddles and stories, and when we were husking corn they'd put a* sandía *in the bottom of the pile, you know, and we had to work fast so we could get to that melon and eat it right there in the moonlight, with all the family and friends around. My father used to make those giant piles of corn in this room, right here, see on the floor there? That's where we'd sit on* pisos *that we'd woven from rags. We'd tell* adivinanzas *and* trabalenguas, *and Papa would tell us stories.*"

"What kind of stories, Grandma?"

"Oh, you know, the same ones I tell you, the cuentos, 'Juan Sin Miedo'—todos esos, *and muchos chistes, too.*"

"And what was your favorite story, Grandma?"

"I liked them all. They really knew how to tell stories in those days, not like today when they just sit around in front of the TV. But I like that one 'Pascual Ranchero,' because it has truths about life, you know? Whoever made those stories was pretty smart.*"

And then Grandma sits down on an old wooden wheel, leans on her knees, tucks her skirt between her legs, and begins her favorite of the old stories. I listen, watching the dust motes float in shafts of sunlight. . . .

ONCE, LONG AGO, there was a priest who lived near the king. There was a long porch on the priest's house where he would walk back and forth every afternoon praying, thinking, saying the rosary. One day the king was looking at him from his balcony and thought to himself, "I guess this priest thinks he's pretty smart. I'm going to find out if he is as smart as he acts."

So the king called one of his servants and sent him to tell the priest that he wanted to see him. The servant went right away, and the priest was very happy that the king had called him. It made him feel *muy importante, muy orgulloso.*

When the priest arrived at the castle, the king said, "I have been watching you for a long time, and it seems you are a very smart man. Let's see if you are as smart as you act. I'm going to ask you three questions, and if you don't answer them within a week, fear for your life!"

Oh, this will be easy, the priest thought. I have many books, and I'm sure that I can find the answer to any question the king can ask.

"The first question is, 'How long will it take me to get to the farthest reaches of the world?'" said the king.

"The second is, 'What is my worth?'

"And the third is, 'What am I thinking?'"

The priest went home right away to study his books and see if he could find the answers to the questions. He looked and looked in every book that he thought could help him, but the answers weren't there. When he realized that he couldn't find them, he began to fear for his life. He decided to run away so the king wouldn't hang him. He went downstairs and told his cook that he was going traveling for a while. By saying that, he thought no one would sus-pect that he was running away and not planning to return.

Early in the morning the priest saddled his horse, and he rode all day. Late that evening he came across a shepherd watching over his sheep.

"Father, what are you doing here?" asked the shepherd.

The priest saw that the shepherd was none other than Pascual Ranchero, the boy who worked for him taking care of his sheep. The priest didn't answer but just shook his head sadly. Right away Pascual Ranchero noticed that something was wrong and said to the priest, "Get down off your horse and come by the fire, Father. Spend the night here with me and rest."

Pascual killed a lamb and roasted some meat on the coals. Then he called the priest to come and eat, but after just one bite he would eat no more. Pascual noticed that the priest seemed preoccupied and asked him, "Why are you so pensive, Father?"

"You know, Pascual," said the priest, "I don't feel very well. I have a stomachache."

"Don't worry about that, Father. I'll get some healing herbs to boil for you," answered the shep-herd. He went off in the pasture and picked some sagebrush and made tea for the priest, but the rem-edy didn't do him any good.

Very early the next day, Pascual Ranchero was up, singing and whistling while he fixed breakfast. The priest thought, "Blessed be God, this lad is so poor and alone and yet so happy, and me, I have every-thing, but I feel so sad."

Pascual called the priest to come and eat, saying, "Look, Father, how good the coffee and the roasted meat are." But the priest wouldn't eat. He kept his eyes fixed to the ground while drawing lines in the dirt.

Finally Pascual said, "Father, you are not sick! You're worried about something and don't want to confide in me. Tell me, Father. Maybe I can help you."

"I am a priest who knows much more than you, and I cannot help myself. What can you do? You are only a poor shepherd," answered the priest.

"You don't lose anything by telling me," said Pascual.

"All right," said the priest. "I'll tell you. It will take a load off my chest, even though you cannot help any other way."

So the priest told Pascual everything, eventually saying, "These questions are so hard, there's no way I can find the answers."

"Well," said Pascual, "what are the questions?"

"You won't have the answers if none of my books did, but if you want to know, here they are," the priest said, and he told Pascual the three questions.

Pascual burst out laughing and said, "You drown in such little water, Father?"

"Don't tell me that you know the answers!" said the priest.

"Yes, I do!" said Pascual.

"Well then, tell them to me!"

"No, I cannot tell you now because the walls have ears and the junipers are very perceptive," said Pascual quietly. "I'll tell you what we will do. Early tomorrow we'll go to your home, and then I'll tell you."

The priest didn't want to go back to the town because he was sure that Pascual didn't know the answers and the king would hang the priest. But at last he agreed to leave the following day. They rode all day down from the mountains and arrived at the priest's home late that night. Pascual went to bed, and as soon as he put his head on the pillow he was fast asleep, but the priest didn't sleep at all.

The next day the priest got up early, but Pascual was still snoring away, very contented, so the priest went to wake him up.

"Pascual, how can you sleep? Aren't you worried?"

"All right, Father, I'll get up, but what's your hurry? The king can wait a while." Pascual got up, stretched, and then said, "Now, Father, you have to trade clothes with me."

"Oh, God! What does this man think he is going to do!" thought the priest. But he was at Pascual's mercy, so, whether he liked it or not, he had to trade clothes with him.

Soon Pascual and the priest left for the king's castle. The people had found out that this was the day that the priest was to appear before their king, and they were all waiting to see if he would hang.

When they entered the castle, the king said to Pascual, thinking that he was the priest, "Come to the front." And to the priest he said, thinking he was speaking to Pascual, "And you, Pascual, sit behind the door."

Then the king asked Pascual, "Father, are you ready to answer the questions?"

"You know what?" answered Pascual. "I have forgotten them! Tell them to me again."

"You forgot them?" exclaimed the king, hardly able to believe what he was hearing.

"I haven't thought about them much," said Pascual, shrugging.

"Well, all right then," said the king. "This is the first one: How long will it take me to get to the farthest reaches of the world?"

Without hesitating even a minute to think, Pascual answered, "If you travel along with the sun, you'll get there in one day."

All the people looked at each other, very surprised, because he had a good answer and the king had to accept it.

"You answered well, very well indeed," said the king. "Now, for the second question: What is my worth?"

Everyone became quiet because they knew that the king thought he was worth a lot of money. If the priest said too little, the king would be mad, but if the priest guessed too much, it would seem like he was calling the king greedy.

"Well, if Jesus Christ was sold by Judas Iscariot for thirty pieces of silver, you are worth nothing," answered Pascual.

Everyone knew that this was the truth. How could a good Christian like the king claim to be worth anything compared to the Savior?

"*Bueno*, Father, that is a good answer," said the king. "But you still have one more question to answer, and if you don't, you will pay with your life. The question is, What am I thinking?"

Pascual just smiled at the king and answered, "Well, Your Highness, I know exactly what you are thinking. You are thinking that I am the priest, but I am Pascual Ranchero, and the person behind the door is the priest!"

The king couldn't do anything but burst out laughing, and the people laughed, too, and then applauded. The priest left the castle contented because everything had come out all right after all.

"Pascual," he said later, "you saved my life, and I don't want you to have to watch over my sheep anymore. I'll get some other boy to do it."

"Father, I appreciate it very much, but I am happier living alone in the mountains taking care of my sheep than I ever would be here in town," answered Pascual. Then he got on his mule and left for the mountains, whistling and singing merrily. ✦

Grandma looks at me over her glasses, smiling. "Dime la verdad, 'jito. Isn't that a good story? I don't know who made it up, but it's true. The people used to have lots of wisdom and say many things that were true, but now? Nada de eso.

"Always my father would save a story like that for the end of the night when we were tired, and afterwards we'd go to bed. If we were tying chiles here on the floor, he would lead us home across the road there, and I remember how we were scared to go out in the night. But the moon was so bright, and we could see a lantern in the window at home, and another at Tío Nicasio's, and we'd get home and the fogones in the corners would be glowing, just embers, you know, and Papa would put us to bed, thinking about how smart that Pascual Ranchero was."

The Land of Mogolló

Haunting landforms surround Chimayó and hold the placitas of the valley in isolation from the outside world. These barrancas, or badlands, are harsh, lonely places that few paths penetrate. In my childhood imagination, this is where the witch lives in the story "The Land of Mogolló." When I hear that story, my childhood mind wanders to the forbidding barrancas beyond the edge of cultivated land, and I'm tempted to go there. But they are across the highway and the Cañada Ancha, and so remain a landscape of fantasy only.

Grandma doesn't share my view. In her mind, and in the minds of those who have told this story over the centuries, land that cannot be cultivated or used for grazing has no value. Its dryness makes the barrancas seem barren, and the vecinos of Chimayó and other neighboring villages find them useless and even frightening.

It's late on Sunday night and the dishes are clean and sit drying on the sink by the open door, where a cool summer breeze stirs. Outside in the darkness, moths circle the porch light and bats chatter and swoop for insects around the lone streetlight. Grandma makes up the bed and I crawl in, sleepy eyed. She puts on her nightclothes and follows, turning off the light. I can hear the water popping and crackling in the water heater in the kitchen. We lie on our backs, side by side.

"Do you want to hear a cuento tonight?" Grandma asks me.

"Yes, yes! 'El Caballero de la Pluma!'"

"No, 'jito , we did that story last night and the night before. I'm tired of that caballero. How about 'La Tierra de Mogolló' ? That's a good story, too. Bueno, lindo, I'm going to tell you that one. You know how you're always fooling around with those lizards? Well, listen to what one of them did once. I tell you, you have to watch out for those creatures!"

ONCE, A LONG TIME AGO, there was a very hard-working man who went every day to the mountains with his burro for a load of firewood to sell in town. He had three daughters and no sons, so he always went to cut wood alone. Yet this man's favorite daughter always wanted to go with him because she loved to go to the mountains to see the *pinavetes*. But going up there was work, not play. So he would tell her, "No, *mi 'jita*, it's far, and I've much work to do. It's no place for a young girl. Today I'm already on my way, but maybe we'll go tomorrow."

One day he was cutting down a pine tree when a big lizard came out from under a stump. The man was scared when he saw the lizard appear, and then the lizard spoke to him.

"I'm going to eat you!" the lizard told him.

"For the love of God," the man begged, "don't eat me!"

"What will you give me if I don't eat you?"

"I am a poor man and have nothing to give you."

"Do you have a family?" asked the lizard.

"I have three daughters."

"Well, I won't eat you if you bring me your favorite daughter tomorrow," the lizard said.

The man went home feeling sad, for he didn't want to give up any of his children, especially his favorite, who reminded him that she was to go to the mountains with him the following day. The next morning the father woke up early to try and sneak out of the house, but his daughter was already up and had prepared food to take to the mountains. So they left for the forest, going to the same place where the lizard had appeared the day before. At first the man didn't see the lizard anywhere and thought, "Perhaps the lizard forgot all about my promise yesterday." But then the man started to cut down a tree, and the lizard appeared as before and crawled up close to him.

The lizard asked, "Did your daughter come with you?" Oh, that lizard was bad, *muy malo*.

"Yes," the man answered. He called to the girl, who was a short way off gathering flowers. "*Mi 'jita linda*," he said, "I have to turn you over to this lizard because if I don't he'll eat me."

The sight of such an ugly animal scared the girl, but, since she was an obedient daughter, she said to her father, "I'll do what you tell me so that this lizard will not eat you." She knew that she had to do whatever her father told her to do, even if she didn't want to go with that lizard.

So the father and daughter said good-bye, and the father went back to his home in the valley feeling sorrowful all the way. When he was out of sight, the lizard turned to the girl and said, "Climb on my back and hold on tightly, but you must close your eyes and not open them until I tell you to!"

The girl did what the lizard commanded. She grabbed that rough, ugly lizard skin and held on tightly, and they disappeared back under the tree stump. Suddenly, the girl felt herself swept up into the sky with the wind rushing past her, like they were flying, and she wanted to open her eyes. Finally, unable to stand it anymore, she peeked and saw the stars overhead and the land far below. Then she closed her eyes tightly again. In a while the lizard told her she could open her eyes, and when she did the girl found herself in a lovely castle with green gardens and flowers all around. It was the most beautiful place she had ever seen.

They arrived late in the day, and it was almost dark. The lizard said to her, "Are you hungry? There is food prepared for you." But the girl wasn't hungry at all. Seeing that she wouldn't eat, the lizard showed her to a big room with a large bed in the middle and a fire roaring in a corner fireplace. She looked around and thought, "How could such an ugly creature become so rich?" She wished she could live in a place like that because she and her father were poor and lived in a tiny house with no windows or furniture.

The lizard talked kindly to the girl so she gradually lost her fear of him, even though he was such an ugly animal. She suddenly felt very tired and lay down to sleep on the bed. The lizard was standing near the fireplace, looking into the flames, waiting for her to fall asleep. When she closed her eyes, he took off the rough lizard skin and became a handsome young man! The girl only was pretending to be asleep and saw everything that happened, and it made her happy to see that the lizard was really a good-looking man. "I'm going to get rid of that ugly skin," she thought as she fell asleep.

The following night the same thing happened. The girl pretended to be asleep again, but this time when the man went to bed she sneaked quietly over by the fireplace, grabbed the lizard skin, and threw it into the fire. It began to crackle and burn with a bright flame, making so much noise that the man woke up.

He jumped out of bed and said, "Oh, no, look at what you have done! Everything is lost!"

"But what's wrong?" asked the girl.

"I am really a prince, and this is my father's castle, but long ago a witch cast a spell on me," explained the prince. "She allowed me to stay here only if I wore that lizard skin during the day, so that no woman would ever see me."

"But so what?" said the girl. "Now we can live together, and I'll be happy because you are a handsome young man."

"No, no. Listen. Now that you burned the skin I will become the witch's prisoner in the Land of Mogolló. I have to go as soon as the sun rises to stay with her in that desolate place."

The prince felt badly because he would have to leave the castle and the girl. Before dawn he woke her and said, "I am sorry to leave you alone, but I'll give you something to remember me by. Perhaps it will help you." He reached in a big chest and pulled out a boot. The prince explained, "This boot will take you wherever you want to go. You only have to say, 'Little boot, take me,' and tell it where you want to go, and it will travel there—and you'll be invisible."

The moment he placed the little boot in her hands the prince and the castle disappeared, leaving the girl all alone in a desert. She felt downhearted and didn't know what to do. She didn't even have her father to help her, and she didn't know which way to go.

"I'm going to look for the Land of Mogolló and find the prince," she finally decided. "But I don't know how to get to that place. Maybe the moon will know, for she is high up in the sky and sees everything." So the girl climbed into the little boot and said, "Little boot, take me to the Land of the Moon!"

The boot quickly took off and flew way up in the sky until they arrived at the Land of the Moon—but the moon wasn't there. Instead, little moons danced all around in the dark, starry sky. The girl asked them, "I'm looking for the Land of Mogolló. Do you know where it is?"

"No," the little moons answered, "but maybe our mother the moon knows. She's traveling on the other side of the earth, but she'll be back soon."

A little while later the moon arrived, shining brightly. "Hello, hello! I smell human flesh around here, and when I find it, I'll eat the little dear!" the moon said. The girl jumped back, scared nearly to death by the big moon.

"No!" the little moons cried. "Don't eat her, for she is only a poor young girl who is looking for the Land of Mogolló. Do you know where it is?"

The moon frowned and thought a moment before saying, "No, I have never seen that place. But I'll bet the sun knows. He travels by day and sees more than I do."

Right away the girl said, "Little boot, take me to the Land of the Sun!" Soon she was in the place where the sun lived, but the sun was away from his home, and there were only little suns, almost like stars, all around. She asked them if they knew where to find the Land of Mogolló.

"We don't know," they answered, "but our father the sun must know, for he travels all around the world. He's on the other side of the world now, but he's coming back soon."

After a while the sun arrived, burning like a big, red fire.

"Hola, hola. A carne humana me huele aquí, y si no me la das, comerte a ti!" said the sun. The girl was scared as before and so hot that she thought she would burn up.

"Don't eat her!" the little suns cried out. "She's only a poor young girl who is in search of the Land of Mogolló. You travel all around the earth by day—don't you know where it is?"

The sun thought a minute and then answered, "No, I have never heard of or seen that place, but perhaps the wind knows, for he travels to the farthest corners of the world and see more than I do."

Without waiting, the girl said to her boot, "Little boot, take me to the Land of the Wind!" The boot went flying until they arrived at where the wind lived. She saw the wind and the little breezes moving all around her and said, "I am looking for the Land of Mogolló. Do any of you know where it is?"

The winds whispered to one another and then answered, "No, we've never heard of such a land, and we travel to every corner of the world. But tomorrow we will all go out looking. Wait here for us, and we will let you know later if we find it."

The next day they all left, and the girl stayed all alone waiting. Just as it grew dark the wind returned—all except one little breeze. They looked very tired and worn out.

"We went to different parts of the world," they told her, "and we looked in every corner, but we didn't find the Tierra de Mogolló."

The girl was very disappointed and thought she would never find the Land of Mogolló. If the moon and the sun and all the wind didn't know where it was, who else could she ask? How could she find it?

Just then the last little breeze arrived. It had been dark for some time, and the wind looked tired and was barely stirring. "I searched for the Land of Mogolló all day and half of the night," the wind whispered to the girl, "and finally I found it beyond the farthest corner of the world. Tomorrow I'll take

you there—if you're sure you want to go to that dreary and lonely place." No one had ever asked to be taken to the Land of Mogolló because it was so far away and lonesome.

"Of course I want to go," the girl said. She hated to think of the prince all alone in such an awful place. So early the next morning when the breezes just began to stir she climbed into the boot and said, "Little boot, follow the breeze to the Land of Mogolló!" The boot took off after the breeze, and they traveled all day until they reached the farthest corner of the world—and then they went even farther. Finally, they arrived at the Land of Mogolló.

It was freezing cold, and there was no light, for the sun and the moon had never shone in the Land of Mogolló. One lonely house stood in that desolate land, and outside the house the witch was getting firewood from a woodpile. She was a mean old witch, and when she heard the breeze she turned her head and said, "Breezes in the Land of Mogolló? Never have I heard them blow!"—for not even a breeze had ever blown there.

"I leave you here," whispered the little wind to the girl. "May all go well with you in this desolate place." And the breeze left the girl alone in the dark outside the witch's house. There was not a living thing in sight—only barren sand and rock and a few coyotes running around.

Soon the old witch went inside the house, and the girl followed her. The girl was invisible, since she was in the little boot, so the witch didn't realize that someone else was with her in the kitchen. She put some wood in the woodstove and then started making *buñuelos*—fritters-cackling to herself as she mixed the dough. The girl watched her from the corner and realized that she was starving, so she tiptoed over to the table and took a *buñuelo*. The witch kept making more, and as fast as she could make them, the girl ate them, until finally the witch exclaimed, "What is this? I keep making *buñuelos* and I can't get ahead!" No matter how fast she made the *buñuelos*, the girl ate them faster.

Finally, the girl filled up and the witch finished a big pile of *buñuelos*. She grabbed a handful of keys and took a plateful with her. The girl followed her in the little boot. They entered a long hallway, and all along the sides there were many little locked rooms. In each one there was a young prince under the witch's spell. The captives looked unhappy in their little rooms but because they were bewitched there was nothing they could do.

The witch went from cage to cage, throwing the *buñuelos* to the men like they were dogs. She laughed when they scurried for the little bits of food because they were so hungry. When the witch came to the last cage, the girl's prince was inside. The girl stayed behind inside the bars, and as soon as the witch went away she climbed out of the boot and appeared. When the prince saw her, he could have died, he was so happy.

"How did you get here?" he asked.

"I followed the witch," the girl said.

"But how did you find the Land of Mogolló?"

The girl told him everything that had happened. Suddenly the prince became dejected. "Why did you come here?" he said quietly to the girl, so the witch wouldn't hear. "Now the witch will find you and cast a spell on you, too, and put you in a tiny cage. You'll be stuck here in this awful Land of Mogolló forever."

"Just tell me how I can get you out of here," the girl said.

"*Bueno*, I'll tell you. There's only one way you can free me," the prince told her. "But it is very dangerous. The witch has two eggs in the *trastero* in the kitchen. Her power is inside these eggs. It will be hard to get near that cupboard, for she guards those eggs carefully. But if you can get there, grab the eggs and break them! That will be the end of the witch."

The next day when the witch went to feed the prisoners, the girl sneaked to the kitchen in her little boot. She had to get out of the boot and climb up onto a chair to reach into the *trastero* where the witch hid the eggs, and as soon as she left the boot she became visible. She opened the cupboard and

just then heard keys jingling and the witch muttering to herself as she returned from feeding the prisoners. The girl hurried, but she had to stand on tiptoes and reach far back in the cupboard—and just then the witch came back in and screamed, "Who are you? And what are you doing in that *trastero*?"

The witch's bony fingers grasped the girl's neck just as the girl got hold of the eggs and threw them on the floor. The moment the eggs broke, the witch fell dead, and the Land of Mogolló became warm and filled with light, for without the power of the witch the sun and moon could shine there again! The girl grabbed the keys and went to let the prince out of his cage.

"How did you kill the witch?" the prince asked excitedly.

"I did just what you told me," said the girl. Then together they opened the doors of the other cages one by one. The princes stepped out and were so happy when they found themselves freed from the witch's evil spell. They started off right away for their own countries, which they discovered were not really so far away. The witch's spell had only made it seem like the Land of Mogolló was beyond the farthest corner of the world.

Finally, the prince and the girl said, "Magic boot, take us back to the castle!" and soon they were in the castle with the gardens all around. "I thought I would never see this place again," said the prince.

The king was overjoyed to see his son and welcomed them. They told the king everything that had happened, and he was thankful to the girl for rescuing his son from the witch's spell. The prince and the girl decided right then to get married and live in the castle—but she hadn't forgotten her father, and first they went to get him so he could live with them.

Her father was cutting wood in the mountains when they found him. He cried with joy when he saw his daughter and said, "I'm sorry that I sent you away with that lizard. I should have let him eat me instead." But when he heard all that had happened, he no longer regretted sending her away.

The girl and the prince celebrated their wedding soon after and lived happily ever after in the castle with the beautiful gardens all around. Her father didn't have to go to the mountains to cut wood anymore—and they all ate quail and hit me on the nose with the bones! ✤

As I drift off to sleep, I ask Grandma, "Where is the Land of Mogolló?"

She motions with her hands toward the north and says, "Acuéstate, lindo."

"And you said to watch out for lizards, but it turned out that the lizard was a prince, Grandma."

"Acuéstate, 'jito!"

"And what was that at the end about quail bones?"

"That's just something my father would say at the end of that story, that's all," she tells me, but I am already slipping off to the barrancas, *peeking over every rise for signs of the* bruja *and her little house. And for many years I hear that witch's voice every time the wind blows in the* barrancas, *saying, "Airecitos en la tierra de Mogolló? Nunca los había visto yo!"*

Old One-Eye

On the south side of the Plaza del Cerro, anchored with talonlike roots to the bank of the irrigation ditch, stands the oldest apple tree I've ever seen. Its few living branches bloom each spring, their snow-white flowers in sharp contrast to the cracked mud walls of my great-great-grandpa José Ramón Ortega's house. This is the archetypal weathered old tree, complete with a hollow on one side that collects rainwater. I imagine the hollow hiding a treasure of gold coins stashed there by the old patrona of the house, Prima Neria, just as El Viejo Tuerto hid his treasure in the cuento Grandma tells me. I imagine that the creaking old house must be full of gold pieces because the size and stature of the great building, with its large, empty rooms and abandoned storefront, bespeaks past wealth.

Grandma's cousins Benjamín and Marcial Ortega come on weekends to tend the orchard of younger apple trees below the house. When these men were young and their father still managed his vast landholdings, the people regarded this as one of the finest orchards in Chimayó, they tell me, and the trees still bear fine crops that they take to Santa Fe to sell. They were among the first red and golden Delicious apples in the valley. Soon most people forgot about the diminutive manzanas mexicanas *that their colonist ancestors had brought to the valley centuries before and instead let those big, juicy apples take over. But this old scarred survivor endures, and a few more* mexicanas *also remain behind Tía Bone's house across the plaza. The small, yellow Mexican apples have no commercial value, but the old people prize them above all others. Grandma promises to bake me some of the* mexicanas *in the fall.*

True to her word, when I'm visiting for an October weekend she takes me and my sister down to Tía Bone's abandoned house, and we fill up a bushel basket with the tiny apples.

"We'll bake these in the oven later," Grandma says, "but they won't come out like they did when we used to bake them in an horno. *There used to be one here." She points to a circle of crumbled adobe in front of the abandoned home.*

We cross the plaza and exit through the narrow opening of the callejón *to get to the old tree by the ditch. Three or four* manzanas *hang from the living branches of the tree, but they're beyond my reach, and Grandma doesn't let me climb the fragile old trunk. I stand back and look at the weathered house and its companion tree, thinking this must be the place where the wise old Viejo Tuerto lived, singing from the back porch here in the twilight.*

"Grandma, this looks like the tree where El Viejo Tuerto hid his money," I say, and Grandma and Prima Neria laugh at me.

"I remember that story!" Neria says. "Mi Tía Bone told it to me once. How does it go, Prima?"

Neria herds us inside to the kitchen table, where she has placed a plate of bizcochitos *and cups of coffee. With the kitchen door open to the golden autumn light outside, Grandma reminds Neria of her youth as she tells us the story of the old man with one eye and a pile of gold coins. . . .*

ONCE THERE WAS AN OLD MAN who was blind in one eye so they called him El Viejo Tuerto, or Old One-Eye. He owned a fig orchard, and every afternoon when it was starting to get dark he went out on his patio to play his violin and sing a little song:

> In the hollow of a fig tree
> *En el hueco de un higuero*
>
> I have two hundred pesos,
> *Tengo mis doscientos pesos,*
>
> In the hollow of a fig tree
> *En el hueco de un higuero*
>
> I have two hundred pesos.
> *Tengo mis doscientos pesos.*

One night there were some boys stealing figs in the orchard, and they heard the song the old man was singing. "What shall we do to scare that old man off so we can steal his money?" they said. "Let's dress up like ghosts and see if that will scare him."

The following night they all came dressed in sheets and approached the old man playing his violin. Together they started singing in a loud voice:

> When we were alive
> *Cuanto hay cuando éranos vivos*
>
> We used to come to steal figs
> *Veníamos a juntar higos*
>
> And now that we are dead
> *Y ahora que somos muertos*
>
> We're coming for El Viejo Tuerto.
> *Venimos por el viejo tuerto.*

When the old man saw them and heard what they were singing, he was so scared that he ran in the house and locked the door. The next day when he went to check on his money in the hollow of the fig tree, there was nothing there. At that moment he realized it was some rascals and not ghosts who had scared him the night before.

"What shall I do so that those thieves will return my money?" he thought. Then he had an idea about how to trick them. As soon as evening came, he sat out on the patio and started to play his violin and sing:

> In the hollow of a fig tree
> *En el hueco de un higuero*
>
> I have two hundred pesos
> *Tengo mis doscientos pesos*
>
> And I'm going to put two hundred more
> *Y con doscientos que voy a poner*
>
> To make four hundred.
> *Son cuatrocientos.*

The same boys were listening, and when they heard what he was singing they said, "El Viejo Tuerto didn't notice that we stole his money! Let's put it back and wait until he puts in two hundred pesos more. That way we will get even more money."

The first thing the next morning the old man went out to see if his money was in the tree. He found it and took it home with him.

That night the boys came back expecting to find four hundred pesos, but instead they found nothing. Then they heard the old man singing from his patio:

> He who wants everything
> *El que todo lo quiere*
>
> Loses everything
> *Todo lo pierde*
>
> He who wants everything
> *El que todo lo quiere*
>
> Loses everything!
> *Todo lo pierde!*

I'm only on my fourth bizcochito *when the story ends. Benjamín and Marcial had entered in the middle of the story, and they sit now, finishing their coffee and getting ready to go back out to the orchard.*

"You know, Tía Bone told me that story one Sunday when my mother and I went to visit her," says Neria. "And she gave me a few reales *afterward to keep. She said I should put them in an apple tree!"*

"Sí, mi Tía Bone, she was always full of stories," says Grandma. "She's the one who told it to me, too. And don't you think that story tells the truth, Prima? That's the way Tía Bone was—always trying to teach us something important. Qué buena que era, no? Wasn't she wonderful?"

Pedro de Urdemalas

Grandma stores her canned fruit, jams, and jellies in the cool of a small adobe build-ing next to the house that we call the dispensita. *They've also moved Grandma's old National woodstove into the* dispensita, *now that she has a modern gas range in the house, but she prefers the old stove for certain tasks—roasting chiles, for example, or occasionally cooking a pot of beans. "No salen en la estufa nueva como salen en esa," Grandma says. And it's true. The pinto beans taste different cooked on the woodstove, and there's no way to roast chiles in a gas range and get the smoky flavor of the wood.*

One summer afternoon the sky is dark with clouds that have been building since before noon. I'm busy with my daily chore of burning the garbage in the incinerator out back—a task I relish for the sheer pyromaniacal joy of it—and the smoldering mass begins to hiss with the first drops of rain. The rumbling of thunder prompts Grandma to call me in from my daily mischief.

"¡Apúrate, 'jito!" Grandma says as I scamper inside and the sky breaks open. "Help me quick, we've got to roast some chiles!"

"Válgame dios!" she mutters and hurries to retrieve some old pots from the stair-way to the attic. When she comes back to the kitchen, we proceed to place the pots in strategic places around the house where we know water will be dripping soon. A scat-tering of pots in the attic, placed there earlier in the summer, will be the first line of defense, but the last rain showed us where water would get past them and through the dirt floor above us.

As the rain becomes heavier, Grandma opens the screen door and tosses a pinch of salt to the sky, along with her protective mantra—"Jesús y cruz!"—then hurries back inside. She grabs one handle of a bushel basket full of green chiles, while I take the other, and we go out into the rain, Grandma holding a scarf over her head. She mutters, "Jesús y cruz!" *several times more as we cross beneath the protective canopy of the trees in the patio and rush into the* dispensita. *Already, rivulets of water flow across the cleanly swept dirt of the yard, gathering up soil and rushing toward the driveway. Rainwater pours off the roof and into the tin basins that Grandma has positioned beneath each* canal *to gather water for washing her hair and for watering the garden. Icy spheres of hail join the rain and start to collect in the gutters.*

The air is dry and warm and faintly dusty inside the dispensita. *Grandma pulls the cord on the single lightbulb overhead and puts the bushel basket on a square wooden table covered with a yellow tablecloth. The green chiles glisten with drops of rain and fill the room with their fresh scent. Grandma reaches to the woodpile and places a stack of split sticks on top of crumpled newspapers in the firebox of the stove. She lets me strike the match and put it to the kindling, and the wood crackles and catches fire.*

While we're waiting for the stove to get hot, I busy myself by looking through the old magazines stacked on the shelf below cans of preserves. In Look, Life, *and the* Saturday Evening Post, *I search out photos of World War II and the numerous grainy images of the JFK assassination, still fresh in our memories. On the walls, torn and faded prints of the Virgin and of Jesus on the cross hang alongside an old medicine cabinet and kerosene lamps. Outside, lightning flashes and thunder roars, and the sound of raindrops on the metal roof is so loud that we can't talk. A muddy torrent rushes down the patio and merges with the overflow from the basins to make a tributary to the river flowing down the road.*

The sweet smell of wet earth wafts through the open doorway as the woodstove finally gets hot enough for roasting the chiles. The rain has quieted to a slow drizzle. We throw handfuls of chiles on top of the woodstove, and they begin to hiss and pop. Now and then we turn them as the room fills with their sharp scent.

"Gracias a dios *that the rain is almost over," Grandma says.*

"I like it when it rains," I respond.

"Oh, sure, the rain is good, but not rain and hail like that. It could have ruined the chiles, like it did last year. I'm glad Tomasita gave us these already, before this rain."

We watch the chiles swell and pop, and it seems to me that we will be here a long time. I tell Grandma that I'm going outside.

"Oh no you aren't. Qué tienes? *It's wet and cold out there, and you could catch a cold. You know, your grandpa went out once . . ."*

"I know, Grandma, and he got sick from the cold and died."

"Bueno, 'jito, I'll tell you a story to pass the time here, about a boy who was muy travieso, *like you. And he was pretty clever, that Pedro de Urdemalas."*

ONCE UPON A TIME there was a woman who had three sons. The oldest was named Manuel, the second one Miguel, and the youngest one Pedro. Everyone called Pedro "Pedro de Urdemalas" because he was such a rascal.

The boys' father had died when the children were young, and their mother had a hard time keeping the family fed. So the sons realized that they had to go in search of work to support themselves and their mother. One day Manuel said to his mother, "Mama, I am going to the king to ask for work so I can earn a few *reales* for you and my brothers."

Everyone knew that this king was mean, and nobody could stand working for him, so no one was surprised when Manuel only lasted one day before returning home. Then Miguel, the second son, decided to try his luck. He went to work for the king, but he, too, only lasted one day and returned home empty-handed. What was worse was that both of the boys had big cuts on their backs where the king had whipped them.

Everyone in the family was discouraged, for they needed to earn some money. But the following day Pedro de Urdemalas said to his mother, "Mama, now it's my turn to work for the king. He will see that he's not going to play around with Pedro de Urdemalas!"

When Pedro arrived at the castle, the first thing the king said to him was, "I can give you work, just like I did your brothers. But there's one thing I am going to tell you right now: You have to obey my orders without question. And another thing," said the king, "neither you nor I will be allowed to get angry with each other. The first one who gets angry will get three strips of flesh torn off his back. If I get angry first, not only will I have three strips of flesh torn off my back, but I will also give you half of my kingdom."

The next day the king ordered Pedro to take the cows to graze in the mountains. No sooner had Pedro left than the king padlocked the gate to the corral. That evening, when Pedro returned with the cows, he saw the locked gate and realized right away that the king was trying to make him mad. But Pedro didn't get angry, and since he was not supposed to question the king's orders, he had to figure out what to do. Finally, he came up with an idea and went to work. He started cutting the heads off all the cows and throwing them into the corral. Then he cut off the legs and threw them in, and so on.

The following day the king went to see what Pedro had done with the cows. When he unlocked the gate and found all the beheaded cows, he almost burst with anger but managed to hold his temper.

"Pedro, what did you do to my cows?" he asked politely.

"Well, I had to throw them over the fence to get them into the corral since the gate was locked. Are you angry about that, Master?" responded Pedro graciously.

"No, no, I am not angry," said the king. "I'm just talking."

The king thought for a moment, planning another way to trick Pedro. Then he said, "By the way, Pedro, I want to warn you that here in the castle we call certain things by names that may be unfamiliar to you. For example, we call the cat 'popurrate.' We call trousers 'childresbildres,' and we call shoes 'garabitates.' I am not called the king but 'reverencia,' and the queen goes by the name of 'fordancia.' Also, we call the castle 'petaca,' fire is 'clarencia,' and water is 'paciencia.' From now on I want you to use these names."

"All right, Reverencia," said Pedro, "I won't forget." The king thought that Pedro would be confused by these strange words, but Pedro was smarter than the king suspected.

When night came and the king and queen went to bed, Pedro caught the cat, wrapped it in rags, set it on fire, and threw it into the room where the king and queen were sleeping. Then Pedro said in a loud voice, "Get up, Reverencia, and you, too, Your

Fordancia! Put on your childresbildres and also your garabitates, for here comes the popurrate, covered with clarencia, and if you don't get some paciencia, your petaca will burn up!"

When the king saw the fire, he became very frightened and screamed at Pedro, "Water, you rascal!"

"Paciencia, Reverencia!" shouted Pedro.

"All right, paciencia it is, but please do what I tell you before the castle burns down!"

"I don't know about castles, but I do know about petacas," answered Pedro.

"Oh, forget about those names I gave you and hurry up and put out this fire!" cried the king in anguish.

At last Pedro put out the fire and asked the king, "Are you angry about what happened, Master?"

The king wanted to yell at Pedro, but he had to say that he wasn't angry. Instead, he began thinking of another way to trick Pedro.

The next day the king told Pedro to fence the orchard, but he didn't give him the materials needed to do it. He thought that surely this would make Pedro mad, but Pedro said to himself, "Well, without any materials to fence I'll have to cut down the trees and use them as fence posts."

So he cut down all the trees in the king's orchard, and when he finished putting up the fence, he went and told the king to come down and see it. The king went to see and found all his trees cut down.

"Why did you do this?" the king asked sadly.

"I had to do it since you didn't give me fence posts," answered Pedro. "Are you angry about it, Master?"

"No, I am not angry. I am just asking," said the king. The king didn't know what else to do to make Pedro mad.

The next day he and the queen left to visit other kingdoms, and they took Pedro with them so he wouldn't get into mischief while they were gone. They had to stop on the road overnight because the first kingdom they were to visit was far away. The king told Pedro to go on ahead and announce to the king and queen of the neighboring kingdom that they would be arriving the next day. He also asked Pedro to make arrangements for food and lodging.

When Pedro arrived at the castle, the servants asked Pedro what the queen's favorite food was. He told them that the only thing the queen liked was plain gruel. The next day, when the king and queen arrived, their hosts were waiting for them with the table laid out with fine linens and bowls of gruel. The king and queen were insulted by this poor meal and wouldn't even taste the soup. Their hosts asked them why they were not eating when they had prepared the queen's favorite food. The king suspected that this was another one of Pedro's tricks to make him angry, so he held his tongue and replied that he and the queen were weary from the long journey and had no appetite. He excused himself and the queen, and they went off to bed hungry.

All night the king lay awake hungry, plotting ways to get back at Pedro and make him angry. By morning he had a scheme. Before going to mass the following day, the king ordered one of his servants to cut the tail off of Pedro's mule. The king was hoping that Pedro would lose his temper when he saw what had been done to his trusted animal.

But when Pedro found his tailless mule, he made a plan of his own. While everyone was in mass, Pedro slipped out and cut the upper lips off of all the king's horses. When the people came out of the church, they saw Pedro sitting outside on the street crying.

"Why are you crying, Pedro?" asked the king. "Are you angry?"

"No, I'm not angry but sad because your horses are laughing at my mule since her tail is chopped off," answered Pedro. The king heard a racket from the stables and went to find out what was going on. When he saw all the horses with their lips gone so they looked like they were laughing, he could barely contain his rage, but he remained silent.

The king didn't know what else to do to get rid of

this rascal, Pedro de Urdemalas. He was desperate and decided to return to his own kingdom instead of proceeding on his journey. On the way back, the entourage camped near a river, and while looking at the rushing water, the king had an idea. "I'll throw Pedro in the river, and that way I'll get rid of him for good!" he thought.

He told the queen of his plan, and in the middle of the night they went to see if Pedro was asleep. But Pedro was awake, for he had heard them whispering and suspected what they intended to do. After that he was watchful every time the king and queen checked on him. Finally, they tired of waiting for him to fall asleep and fell asleep themselves. Pedro then went and carefully took the queen in his arms, carried her to his bed, and lay down next to the king.

Early in the morning, when it was still dark, the king woke up and whispered to Pedro, thinking that he was the queen, "Look! Pedro has finally gone to sleep. Let's go and throw him in the river!"

Pedro didn't say a word but followed the king and helped him throw the queen into the river. They watched her float down the river. Then as they were walking back to the camp the king said, "At last we are going to live in peace without that Pedro de Urdemalas."

Pedro answered matter-of-factly, "You are talking to Pedro, Master."

When the king realized that he had thrown the queen into the river instead of Pedro, he started crying and then yelled at Pedro, "Go ahead and tear the flesh off of my back! I am not only angry but very sad. As soon as we reach the castle, I will give you half of all my kingdom if you will just leave me in peace!"

So Pedro went back home loaded with money. With the fortune that he had gained, Pedro and his mother and his brothers lived happily the rest of their lives. ✛

The last chile is "sweating" beneath a white cloth in the bushel basket. The heat from the woodstove has become oppressive, and I chafe to be outside. We carry the basket back to the house, where Grandma will peel the chiles and put them in bags to freeze.

"You can't help me peel these," she says. "Remember last time you got chile in your eye? Go on now and play."

And I run down to the ditch to capture water striders and snakes.

Juan Rodajas

"I have fallen twenty-six times in my life," Grandma tells me as she washes out a scrape on my knee from my latest tumble. We're sitting on the benches in her patio, in the shade of a giant locust tree in full bloom. The bunches of white flowers hang like grapes and fill the air with a sweet fragrance.

"How can you remember every time that you fell?" I ask.

"I can still feel them all. The worst fall gave me this maturanga *in my back, right here," she says, rubbing her lower back. She puts my hand on it, and I'm fascinated by the cool, tough knot, a miniature version of the swollen lump on Prima Neria's twisted spine. I mention the similarity, and Grandma says, "Ah, no, 'jito, my little* herida *is nothing compared to that poor woman's back. That happened when a wagon rolled over her, but this came from the time I fell down the stairs in Durango. Ay, cómo me duele. It sure hurts."*

I had recently fallen down the stairs myself, and I remind Grandma, showing her my toothless grin.

"I know you fell, 'jito, I was there. But in Durango I fell much further, and I was already grown up, when it hurts more. It was winter, and oh those winters up there were cold. But that morning I got up early. Your mother was just a baby and was in bed with us. The room was cold, and we needed some coal for the stove, but I decided to let your grandpa stay in bed and play with Stella, and I went out for the coal. Ah, qué tonta! How could I be so foolish? I put on my robe and a hat and walked out on the porch. We lived on the second story, above the grocery store that my father-in-law owned, so we had to climb up and down these outside stairs for everything. It was awful. I stepped on the first step, which was covered with ice, and there I went, tumbling down about twenty stairs, head over heels all the way to the bottom, like Juan Rodajas. When I stopped, I couldn't even move. And your grandpa was lying in bed warm and happy, not even knowing what happened."

"You rolled like Juan Rodajas?" I say, laughing, and Grandma laughs, too, even though she says it's not funny. The image of her rolling down the stairs stays with me, and for years I remind her of Juan Rodajas whenever she recounts all the times she has fallen.

ONCE THERE WAS A YOUNG MAN who went by the name of Juan Rodajas, or Rolling Juan, because instead of walking like most people he got around by rolling. Every day he would go to the forest and return rolling down the road with a load of firewood.

One day, when Juan Rodajas finished cutting his load of wood for the day, he sat under a pine tree to rest and have a bite to eat. As he was sitting there eating his loaf of bread, an old man appeared and said to him, "Why don't you give me a piece of your bread?"

"With pleasure," answered Juan Rodajas without hesitating. Then he cut the loaf and gave half to the old man.

"You're a generous lad," said the old man. "And for that reason I am going to reward you with this magic wand. It will give you whatever you ask, if you ask in the right way. Just say these words: 'Magic wand, by the power that you have and that God has given you, grant me this wish.'"

Juan thanked the old man and made his way home, rolling down from the mountain into town. He arrived home tired and hungry and lay down to rest. He was trying to think of something to make for supper when he remembered the wand that the old man had given him. He pulled the wand from his pocket and said, "Magic wand, by the power that you have and that God has given you, make a table appear before me with every kind of food that God has made."

As soon as he said those words, there appeared a table heaped with all the kinds of food one could ever desire. Juan, being a poor man, had never seen so much food in all his life, and he ate with delight all that was before him.

Now it so happened that the road that Juan followed to the woods each day passed by the king's castle, and one day when Juan was rolling down the road with his load of firewood, the princess was sitting out on the balcony. When she saw Juan go rolling by, she burst out laughing.

Juan was ashamed, but then he thought, "The princess is very haughty and laughs at me. I'll show her!"

When he was out of sight of the castle, Juan took the magic wand out of his pocket and said, "Magic wand, by the power that you have and that God has given you, make the princess get pregnant without knowing it."

The princess was no longer laughing when, after nine months, she had a baby. Since she wasn't married, the king was angry with his daughter and demanded to know who had fathered the child.

"I swear to you, Father, I don't know how I became pregnant," the princess cried. But the king didn't believe her. He sent out an order to all the men in his kingdom, demanding that every one of them appear before him so that he could find out who the baby's father was. One after another, all the men came and stood before him, but none resembled the child at all. Perplexed and angrier than ever, the king paced around the castle all night long.

In the morning one of the king's servants came to see him. He knelt before the throne and said, "Your Majesty, I know of one man who did not appear before you yesterday. His name is Juan Rodajas."

"Juan Rodajas!" exclaimed the king. "It's not possible that my daughter would pay any attention to that man who doesn't walk like other men. But if you are certain he is the only man left in my kingdom, then go get him for me!"

When the servant came to his door, Juan told him that he would be glad to visit the king. He went right to the castle and rolled up to the gates. All the townspeople watched him and were amazed that the king would call him. The gates of the castle swung open, and Juan entered. There in the courtyard stood the king and the princess with her baby. As soon as the baby saw Juan, he started screaming, "Papa! Papa!"

The princess blushed and said to the king, "Surely you don't think that Juan Rodajas is the father of my child?"

"You must leave my castle today," answered the king angrily. "You have shamed me and all the royal family. Go with Juan Rodajas and your baby. I never want to see you again."

The poor princess left the castle crying and followed Juan Rodajas as he rolled down the road to his house. People along the roadway laughed and talked about them as they passed.

The next day the princess woke up in her new home. Early in the morning, Juan left for firewood while the princess stayed with her baby in the one-room hut. Since the princess was accustomed to having a maid come and help her with everything, she scarcely knew how to dress herself, much less cook and feed her child. She began to cry because there was no food prepared for them.

That night when Juan came back from the mountains, the princess and the baby were asleep. They hadn't eaten all day. Juan reached into his pocket and took out the magic wand. Speaking softly so the princess wouldn't hear him, he said, "Magic wand, by the power that you have and that God has given you, set me a table with all kinds of food that God has made." Instantly the table appeared, and he woke the princess. She was astonished to see the feast, but she was too tired to ask questions. The three ate their fill and then ate some more. Even at the castle the princess had never had such good food.

The next day the same thing happened. Juan came rolling home and made a feast appear while the princess slept. But this time the princess opened one eye while she pretended to sleep, and she saw Juan take the magic wand out of his pocket. She listened closely to every word that he said.

The next night the princess waited for Juan to go to sleep, and then she took the wand out of his pants pocket. When Juan left for wood in the morning, she went for the wand and said, "Magic wand, by the power that you have and that God has given you, make a beautiful house appear, with furnishings more splendid than those of the king. And also the most luxurious apparel for me. And clothes fit for a prince for Juan and my child." She thought a minute and then added, "And please make Juan walk upright like other men!"

Instantly the magic wand granted the princess all that she asked for. That night, Juan came down the road walking upright with his bundle of wood tied to his back. "There goes Juan Rodajas," the other woodcutters said. "But he's not rolling anymore. What a miracle!"

As time passed, the princess and Juan grew accustomed to living a good life. Whenever they needed anything, they just took out the wand and would lack no more. They had the finest clothes, a grand house, all the best foods, and Juan no longer had to cut wood in the mountains. The princess was happy, and the child was growing up to be a fine young boy.

After a while the princess decided it was time to ask her father to come to dinner. The king was glad to accept the invitation, for he had heard that there was a house in his kingdom that was as beautiful as his castle.

The king went to the house, escorted by all of his servants. When he arrived, Juan opened the door to receive him, but the king didn't recognize Juan because he was dressed in elegant clothes and walked like other men. The princess also made sure she dressed so that the king wouldn't recognize her either.

The princess had told the wand to set a table with the best food imaginable. The king, Juan, the princess, and the child ate breads and meat and potatoes and gravy and desserts that were the sweetest in the world. Never in his life had the king eaten such good food. He was quite surprised and couldn't help but wonder how these people had acquired such wealth, for he had always had the most money in the entire kingdom.

When they finished eating, the king asked Juan, "Who is your father to have given you such wealth?" Juan told him his parents' names, but the king had never heard of them since they were not among the royalty he had known in his life.

Soon the princess went to another room and asked the wand, "Magic wand, by the power you have and that God has given you, make the king take my gold ring home inside his right shoe." Then she went back into the dining room, where they continued conversing until it grew late. At last the king thanked his hosts for the wonderful meal and left with his servants and their horses. But no sooner had the king returned to his castle than a messenger from the princess arrived.

"What do you want?" asked the king. "I am tired and want to rest."

"My mistress sent me to tell you that she wishes to see you as soon as possible."

The king could not imagine why the lady wanted to see him, but he agreed to go. "Perhaps they will tell me where they acquired such wealth," he thought.

When the king arrived at the princess's house, she told him, "Thank you for coming back, Your Majesty. I called you to tell you that I am missing my gold ring, and I think that you have taken it."

"Are you accusing me of being a thief!" exclaimed the king, very angry.

"I think you have my ring in your shoe," answered the princess.

"Nonsense," said the king. "Why would I take your ring and hide it in my shoe?"

"Take off your right shoe, and let's see," ordered the princess.

The king took off his right shoe, and the ring fell out on the floor. He was surprised and told the princess, "But how is it possible that I had that ring in my shoe without knowing how it got there?"

"Do you know who I am?" asked the princess. "I am your daughter, whom you banished from your castle, and just like you were carrying that gold ring in your shoe without knowing it, I became pregnant without knowing it."

When the king heard all this, he begged his daughter's forgiveness and asked that she, Juan, and the child come live with him in his castle.

"I forgive you," said the princess. "And I thank you for inviting us to live with you, but we are happy here in our own home."

Over the years the magic wand continued to give Juan, the princess, and their child everything that their hearts desired, and they lived happily all their lives. ✛

I'm staring up into the locust blossoms as the story ends. "Go on now, and be careful," Grandma says. "I'll sew that tear in your pants later. Just try and walk upright, like other boys, from now on, eh?"

Over the years, Grandma adds more falls to her life list. But even when, at the age of ninety, she falls across the bathtub and is unable to get up by herself, no bones are broken, although she does start to use a cane. By ninety-six, she must use a walker, then a wheelchair, to get around. She chafes at the increasing limitations and fights against her diminishing capabilities. Worst of all for her is her inability to work in the kitchen, making meals and bizcochitos for guests.

One day when she is one hundred years old, I am taking her to the eye doctor for a checkup, and as I roll her across the parking lot in her wheelchair she says, "Here I go, rolling along like Juan Rodajas again!"

Fearless John

The kitchen door and the window by the big double bed are open. A cool breeze stirs the curtains with the scent of rain from a heavy summer sky as I stare up at the image of the infant Jesus on the wall above me, hanging crookedly on the cracked wall. I can just hear the gurgling of the waters in the Acequia de los Ortegas behind Papa Reyes's house across the road—the very place where Grandma first heard the cuentos as a child.

The aroma of chile and fried potatoes lingers in the house, and thunder rumbles and roars in the distance, coming closer by the minute. Over the jagged edges of the barrancas, strange lights flicker as if in a faraway world while cricket songs pulse in the lilacs, reminding me of the bells the dancers wear at the pueblos. Grandma bustles around getting ready for bed and then sits beside me to put me to sleep. I feel afraid of the thunder and the approaching rain, and Grandma senses it.

"Bueno, lindo, antes de dormir, let's say our prayers," Grandma says, and together we recite:

> Con Jesús me acuesto
> Con Jesús me levanto
> Con la virgen María
> Y el Espíritu Santo
> Quién da luz en esta casa?
> Jesús.
> Quién la llena de alegría?
> María.

Quién la llena de fe?

José.

Cuan claro se ve

Teniendo en corazón

A Jesús, María, y José . . .

Grandma climbs into her side of the bed. "I can tell you are sleepy," she says, pointing her finger at me. "Acuéstate. Tonight we'll have just a short cuento, bueno? But don't have any fear now, lindo. We are safe. No one is going to hurt us. What is there to fear?"

I know by her last line that Grandma is going to tell the story of the boy who had no fear, Juan Sin Miedo. With the first words of the story, my anxiety about the approaching storm outside recedes. . . .

ONCE THERE WAS A YOUNG MAN named Juan, who since he was a little boy had feared nothing. While other small children frightened easily and ran from any kind of loud noise or barking dog, Juan would just smile and keep on doing whatever he was doing. "What is there to fear?" he would ask. Because of this, his family and everyone in town began to call him Juan Sin Miedo, Fearless Juan.

One day when Juan was a young man he told his mother that he was going to look for work with the king. His father had died in the mines when Juan was a baby, and life was very hard for them. "It's time for me to earn some money so we can live a better life," Juan told his mother.

She didn't want Juan to leave, but she knew they needed money to buy food and things for the house, so she let him go. "All right," said Juan's mother, "go and look for work in the world. But be very careful of those men who roam the roads doing evil deeds! *Entiendes?*"

But Juan didn't care. "What is there to fear?" he said and gathered his few belongings to take with him on his trip. His mother prepared some chicken and biscuits for him to take along. When other boys

in town heard that Juan was going to look for work with the king, they came from their houses to join him, with the same purpose in mind.

The boys walked all day long. Then just as it was getting dark they came upon an abandoned house that looked scary, with the windows all broken and the roof falling down. Some of the boys said they should keep going until they found a house with someone home, but Juan just shrugged and said, "What is there to fear? Since it's late, let's spend the night here."

The others consented, and they walked across the old, wooden portal and pushed open the creaking door. Bats flew from the *vigas* and off into the moonlight. Despite this, the boys lay on the floor of packed mud to rest.

A little while after they had settled down there was a loud racket on the roof. "What was that!" some of the boys shouted, and they all ran for the door. "Oh, don't worry about it," said Juan, "what is there to fear?"

The boys respected Juan for his fearlessness, so they wrapped themselves in their *cobijas* and lay down again on the floor. No sooner had they closed their eyes than they heard the noise again, and this time a deep, moaning voice as well. At this, the boys jumped up and ran out the door, leaving Juan all alone. Muttering "What is there to fear?" he rolled over and sat up.

"All this commotion has made me hungry," he said, and he took out his chicken and biscuits and started eating as if nothing was wrong. As he was munching on his supper, he again heard the banging on the *latillas*. Then there was a deep, mournful voice that said, "*Caigo! Caigo!* I'm falling down! I'm falling down!"

"Oh," said Juan, looking up at the rotting *latillas*. "Go ahead and fall, but don't ruin my chicken!"

Pieces of the ceiling fell down in a cloud of dust, and then a human leg bone dropped from the ceiling and nearly struck Juan. He grabbed it and threw it in the corner where he had been throwing the chicken bones. Then he kept on eating.

In a few minutes the voice began crying out again, "*Caigo! Caigo!* I'm falling down! I'm falling down!"

"Can't you see I'm trying to eat?" said Juan. "Come on down, then, but just don't fall on my chicken!"

At that, another leg bone fell from the ceiling and landed right next to Juan. He threw it in the same corner where he had thrown the other one. The voice called out again, and down came the kneecaps. With the next cry came the anklebones, then the toes, the pelvis, the ribs, and so on until finally the skull came tumbling down, crying out, "*Caigo! Caigo!*" as it crashed to the floor. When Juan threw the skull with the other bones, the entire skeleton came together and stood up in the corner.

Juan looked at the skeleton but just kept on eating his chicken and biscuits as if nothing out of the ordinary had happened. The skeleton stared at Juan for a while and then spoke, saying, "Dig there!" while pointing to the floor with a long, bony finger.

"*Cansado y muerto de andar y viene esta esquele-to aquí a mandar,*" Juan shouted. "Here I am tired

and half dead from traveling, and here comes this sickly looking creature to order me around!" said Juan, scowling at the skeleton.

"Dig there!" the skeleton insisted.

"All right, if you promise you will let me eat in peace, I'll do what you say," answered Juan, and he started digging in the dirt floor. In a little while he hit something hard, and when he dug it out he discovered that it was an earthen jar. He dusted off the top and opened it, finding that it was full of gold coins.

"Here you are! Is this what you wanted?" said Juan, and he handed the jar to the skeleton. "Now, I'm tired and want to go to sleep."

Juan threw his *sarape* over himself and lay down on the floor. The skeleton walked over to him and said, "You take this money. I want you to use it to pay for ten masses for me so I can get into heaven. Whatever money that is left over is yours."

"All right, whatever you say," said Juan, and he placed the jar beside him and went to sleep, not the least bit worried about the skeleton that stood grinning beside him.

The next day when he woke up Juan went to the priest in the town just down the road and said, "Father, I want you to say ten masses for the repose of the soul of the man who once lived in the abandoned house down the road. I can pay you for them right now." Then Juan took out the jar and gave the priest a handful of coins.

When the priest saw the glittering gold, he wanted all of it for himself. So he thought of a way that he could get it from Juan. "Come into this room, my friend," said the priest, and he led Juan to a small room with no windows. He opened the door for Juan, and when Juan entered he slammed it behind him and locked it. In a little while, Juan's eyes began to get used to the dim light, and he saw what was all around him. It was a room full of skeletons and skulls! The priest was hoping that Juan would die of fear in that room, leaving the money for him.

In the morning the priest went to see if Juan had

died of fright. He opened the door, and there was Juan playing ball with the skulls! "Catch this!" shouted Juan, and he threw a skull at the priest. The priest jumped back, and the skull rolled to his feet, smiling up at him.

"*Buenos días le de Dios,*" said Juan politely. "Thank you for putting me up for the night. This is a nice room."

Finally the priest realized that Juan was not going to be frightened. "Now I know why they call him Juan Sin Miedo," he thought. He asked of Juan only enough money for the masses and then said ten masses for the departed soul of the man who had owned the abandoned house. Juan went to every service and during this time stayed in the abandoned house. Only after the tenth mass did the skeleton stop moaning all night long and pacing up and down the floor.

After the masses Juan went back home. His mother was surprised to see him coming down the road after such a short time away. She ran out to greet him and asked if he had found work. "No, Mama, I don't have to worry about work anymore," Juan said. Then he showed her the jar of money and told her the story of what had happened.

"But what if that money belongs to someone else and they come for it? What if that skeleton comes to try and take it back?" Juan's mother asked him, very worried.

"What is there to fear?" said Juan.

Soon Juan called a carpenter and paid him with gold pieces to build a beautiful house for himself and his mother. Even after spending money on the house, he had enough left over for them to live in comfort for the rest of their lives. ✜

Grandma finishes the cuento and then adds:

Una vez había un gato
Con las patas de trapo
Y los ojos al reves
Quieres que lo cuento otra vez?

I know that if I answer yes, she'll repeat the verse, so I say nothing, and as I'm falling asleep I think of skeletons and skulls and remember that numerous ancestors are buried beneath the floor in the Santuario and the local chapel. I imagine the cool, dark interiors of those buildings and can see myself as Juan Sin Miedo, catching leg bones of dead relatives and tossing them into the corner.

María Linda

Whenever she can find us a ride, Grandma takes me to mass at the Santuario early on Sunday mornings. She wears a black mantilla *and becomes uncharacteristically somber when we enter the Santuario. We take our places in the pews and bow our heads before the manifold images of Christ, the Virgin, and the saints painted on the reredos. Father Roca, the Catalán priest from Barcelona, presents the liturgy in Spanish, his thick accent making it difficult for a child struggling to comprehend Spanish. The foreignness and unintelligibility of his speech evoke for me the same mysterious atmosphere that the Latin Mass once did.*

The dark interior of the Santuario and the relentless suffering shown in the artwork terrify me. These images bear no resemblance to those of the same saints that I'm familiar with in the church we belong to in Los Alamos. The depictions here have a raw quality that reveals a true understanding, if not an obsession, with suffering and self-abnegation. The knowledge that some of my ancestors are buried in the floor beneath my knees adds to my sense of awe.

After the mass, we cross in front of the altar, genuflecting before Our Lord of Esquipulas and the elaborate altar screen. We duck through the tiny side door and go to el pocito—the place where my great-grandfather five times over, Bernardo Abeyta, is said to have found the buried crucifix that inspired the construction of the church. We pray and take a pinch of holy dirt from the hole in the floor. The rows of flickering candles warm the room and rob it of oxygen, and I feel giddy as we kneel on the packed dirt floor. When I stare at the numerous bultos *around me, the wall full of crutches and canes in the next room—left by those who were healed by the holy dirt—and the portraits of loved ones departed or in pain, I feel overwhelmed with sadness. Yet it is a sadness that I'm taught to embrace as the essence of being spiritual, for suf-*

fering is the road to redemption. "Tiene uno que sufrir para merecer," Grandma whispers to me as she lights a candle.

As we leave the interior of the Santuario, Father Roca greets us in the courtyard, and we visit while he blesses parishioners and tourists alike. I steal away and walk down to the river below the church to kneel by the clear, flowing stream and splash water on my face to relieve the feeling of lingering faintness.

It was right at this spot that Grandma's cousin, Ramón Quintana, came walking down from the hills after being lost for days in the mountains—a miraculous event credited to the spiritual power of the Santuario. The story goes that Primo Ramón was lost as a child when his family was gathering piñon nuts in the mountains. After days of fruitless searching, his parents gave him up for dead and went home to Santa Cruz filled with grief. Days later, Ramón walked out of the hills, following this river, and showed up at the Santuario barefoot, with his shoes in his hand. When pressed for an explanation of how he found his way down from the sierra, Ramón explained that a kind woman dressed in blue had taken him by the hand and led him down the river from the mountains all the way to the Santuario. In gratitude for seeing her son alive and well, Ramón's mother made a promesa to make a pilgrimage back to the Santuario each year on Good Friday, a vow she kept all her life and one that Ramón also fulfilled.

I find the story of Ramón and the Virgin more uplifting than being in church, and I ask Grandma to tell it to me over and over. Whenever she does, I can vividly see the child Ramón coming down from the hills, led along the river to Chimayó by the Virgin where I, too, have walked. It reminds me of the apparition of the Virgin that also appeared to María Linda in the Northern New Mexican version of the Cinderella story that Grandma tells. . . .

ONCE, LONG AGO, there was a man who had one daughter named María Linda. This man was a widower, and he and María lived alone. The woman next door had also lost her spouse and had only one daughter. María Linda liked to visit this neighbor because the woman always gave her a piece of bread dipped in honey. In fact, María Linda was so fond of the woman that one day she said to her father, "Papa, why don't you marry our neighbor? She is so good to me. She gives me bread dipped in honey every time I go over there."

María Linda's father had to admit that he was lonely and missed having a wife in the house, and he had long suspected that the widow wanted to marry him, but he was worried about how the woman would treat María Linda later. He warned María Linda, "Today she gives you bread dipped in honey, *mi hijita,* but tomorrow she will give bread dipped in bile." But María Linda wouldn't listen to her father, and she pestered him so much that he finally married the neighbor.

Just as her father had warned, they had lived together only a little while when María Linda's new stepmother began to treat her badly. She made María Linda do all the housework while her own daughter did nothing but clean her nails and change into different dresses every day. But even though she was dressed in rags María Linda was beautiful, and the stepmother and daughter were jealous of her. So they began to plan ways to make trouble for her.

María Linda had a lamb that she had taken care of since its birth, and one day, just to be cruel, the stepmother told María Linda's father to kill that lamb. Now, they killed and ate their animals from time to time, and to slaughter the lamb was not so unusual since everyone enjoyed roasted lamb for dinner. But María Linda's father knew how much his daughter loved this particular lamb, and he didn't want to do it. Finally, though, just to keep peace with his wife he did what she ordered.

The father skinned the lamb properly and cleaned it for roasting. He saved nearly every part of the lamb, including the intestines, which they commonly used to make *burriñates,* one of María Linda's favorite foods. Then the stepmother sent María Linda to wash the animal's intestines, and María Linda went down to the river crying because her stepmother was so cruel. While María Linda was washing the intestines, some fell into the water. As she stood there crying and watching the entrails float down the river, a lady dressed in blue and wearing a crown of twelve stars appeared before her.

"Why are you crying, my child?" she asked.

"Because they have killed my lamb, and now, to make it worse, I lost some of the *tripas* in the river," answered María Linda.

"Don't cry," said the lady. "I'll get them back for you. But listen. Over there in that house is a little baby. Go see him while I fetch the *tripas.*"

María Linda went to the house and found a baby crying and dirty. The house was a mess, with clothes and dishes lying all around. María Linda took the baby in her arms and consoled him until he stopped

crying. She fed and bathed the child and put him to rest. After that she cleaned up the house and then went back to the river.

"How was the baby?" asked the lady.

"He was crying and all dirty, so I gave him a bath and put him to sleep. Then I cleaned the house."

"Here are the *tripas* that fell in the river, and here is your reward," said the lady, smiling.

She tapped María Linda on the forehead, and a beautiful star appeared, shining as brightly as the sun.

When María Linda returned home, her father, stepmother, and stepsister asked her how she had ended up with a star on her forehead. María Linda told them all that had happened by the river. The stepsister became jealous of the star and wanted one for her own forehead. So she asked her stepfather to kill another lamb, and she went to clean the intestines in the river, just like María Linda had done.

While she sat by the riverbank, hurriedly splashing the *tripas* in the river, she deliberately let some fall into the current. As they were swept away, she pretended to cry. Right away the woman dressed in blue appeared and said, "What are you doing, my child?"

"Oh, some of the intestines fell in the river, and I am looking for them," answered the girl.

"I'll look for them. You go to that house over there, where you will find a baby. See how he is."

The girl went and found the baby crying and all dirty. She became impatient and angry with the infant. After looking around the house for a minute, she gave the baby a good spanking and left him crying, just the way she had found him. Then she hurried back to where the woman in blue was waiting.

"How was the baby?" asked the lady.

"Oh, he was crying and dirty, so I gave him a good spanking and left him crying. That should teach him!"

"All right, my child, here are the intestines, and here is your reward," said the lady.

She tapped the girl lightly on the forehead, and

right away a big horn grew there. The girl started for home, happy because she thought that she had a star on her forehead just like María Linda.

The girl's mother gasped when the girl came through the door. She was angry because now her daughter was more unattractive than ever. She exclaimed, "Why have you come back with a horn instead of a star like María Linda? Didn't you do what María Linda did?"

When the girl told her what she had done with the house and the child, the mother could not say anything because she realized that she had taught her daughter to be selfish and mean. She grabbed a saw and cut the horn off the girl's forehead, but she had to leave a piece protruding. So to hide the stump she fixed the girl's hair in curls that hung down low over her forehead.

Now the stepmother and her daughter were even meaner to María Linda. They never let her go out anyplace because she was even more beautiful than her stepsister, especially now that she had a star on her forehead while the stepsister had the stump of a horn.

Time passed, and one day the king announced that he was giving a ball for his son, the prince, so that the prince could meet the young ladies of the kingdom and choose one to be his bride.

When the day of the celebration came, the step-mother and her daughter spent all day getting ready. They bought the finest clothes and stayed in front of the mirror for hours, fixing their hair and putting on makeup. When they went to the ball, they left María Linda home alone, cleaning the house as ususal.

María Linda began to cry, and then the lady dressed in blue appeared to her again and asked, "What's the matter? Why are you crying?"

"Because my stepmother and her daughter went to the ball that the king is giving for the prince, and they didn't invite me," answered María Linda.

"Don't worry about that. Ask whatever you wish, and I will grant it to you," said the lady.

So María Linda asked for a dress that would be more beautiful than anybody had ever seen, a pair of golden slippers, and a carriage and horses to take her to the ball. Right away the lady in blue moved her hand through the air, and all these things appeared. María Linda was so happy she jumped into the carriage and rode down the road toward the castle.

As soon as she got to the castle, the prince saw María Linda. He was enchanted with her smile and with the pretty golden star on her forehead, and he asked her to dance right away. He danced only with her the rest of the night, and while they danced he asked her many questions. But María Linda didn't want to tell him who she was because she knew her stepmother would be angry. When it got late, she turned away from the prince and went running out of the ballroom, accidentally dropping one of her slippers as she left. The prince ran after her and picked up the golden slipper.

The next morning the prince went out early to look throughout the kingdom for the girl whose foot would fit the slipper. When he came to the house where María Linda and her family lived, right away the stepdaughter came out to try on the slipper. She jammed her foot into the little shoe, but no matter how hard she tried she couldn't make it fit. Disappointed, the prince asked, "Isn't there anyone else here who could try on this slipper?

"No," said the stepmother, "I have only one daughter."

Just at that moment, María Linda's cat came out and started to cry, "*Miao, Miao, María Linda está en el estrado.* Meow, Meow, María Linda is in the attic."

"What did that cat say?" asked the prince.

"It was nothing," answered the stepmother, hurriedly kicking the cat under the table. But the cat kept meowing, louder now, "*Miao, Miao, María Linda está en el estrado.*"

The prince got down on his knees to hear the cat better, and finally he made out what it was saying. Surprised, he asked, "Who is this María Linda?"

"Oh, she is just our servant girl. Don't pay her any mind," answered the stepmother.

"Well, bring her here so she can try on the slipper, too," ordered the prince.

"But she's ugly, and I'm sure that the slipper wouldn't fit her big feet. They're full of calluses from so much work—not so fine as my daughter's pretty little feet."

The prince grew suspicious and insisted on seeing María Linda. Like it or not, the stepmother had to bring María Linda out of the attic, where they had locked her up. María Linda tried on the slipper, which fit perfectly. Then she took the other slipper out of her dress pocket, where she had hidden it, and the prince saw that it matched the one she'd dropped at the ball. And when he looked at her face, he saw the golden star.

The prince scolded the stepmother for her cruelty, saying, "All along you hid this girl's beauty from the world. It will remain locked behind closed doors no more!" Then he announced he would take María Linda with him back to the castle. She insisted that they take her father, too, who was sorry that he had brought the cruel stepmother into their lives. Soon after, the prince and María Linda were married. They had a great feast and invited all the people of the kingdom—except the mean stepmother and her daughter. After the dinner, they had a ball, and the prince and his new princess danced all night. ✣

Many years after I first heard the story of María Linda, I am still coming to the Santuario, drawn more by the sparkling river and the sight of the green potreros *than by the shadowy church interior with all its weighty symbolism. Now, a high steel fence keeps me from the river, though, and diminishes the sense of connection between the church and the landscape. Also, the road to the church has been paved and a nearby field leveled to make room for the cars that carry the thousands of pilgrims who come here for the church's holy dirt.*

Inside, pilgrims still fall on their knees before the reredos, *but now the paintings are lit brightly by flood lamps, and somehow the light lessens the mystery that pervaded the room when I was a child. Whereas we knelt on a dirt floor beside rickety old benches, today there are finely crafted wooden benches with padded kneeling bars, and the floor is paved with flagstone. Few are the veiled women who come here these days, and they are greatly outnumbered by tourists with cameras who point noisily at the artwork. But the Santuario's somber atmosphere still casts a powerful spell that pushes me outside to the light of day, where I can reflect on the simple miracles wrought in the hills near the river by the lady dressed in blue.*

The Three Little Oxen

Grandma doesn't like to talk about brujería, but I hear people gossip about witches in Chimayó and ask Grandma if she ever knew of any. She always changes the subject, even when I remind her that witches make appearances in some of her cuentos. It takes a lot of pestering to break her down.

"Bueno, lindo, I'll tell you about some witches I heard of just so you'll stop bothering me. But I never heard of them around here. No, the vecinos of the Plaza del Cerro here, they didn't believe in those things. But a few miles away, I heard there was a witch, and I'm sure it's true because my primos who live there said it was true.

"See, there was this partera—midwife—and they thought she was a witch because she used to go around with this group of women, and they'd go out late at night and come home very late, in the early morning. And one night when she was out, this man, he heard a racket out by his chicken coop, and when he went out there was a big owl there, and he shot at it but it flew away.

"Well, the next morning this woman came out of her house with a white cloth wrapped around her head, and she wore it every day after that. Someone saw her take that rag off one time, and there beneath it was a big hole in her head, open and with blood and everything. That was the wound from the shotgun! See, witches turn into owls at night, and she was the owl that the man shot. And the rest of her life she wore that rag. I saw her myself, and they say she never went out without it. So I guess it's true she was a bruja.

"Then there was another time there was this man from down below there, and he fell in love with a woman who was a witch. This man was already married, you know, but he started going around with this witch, and soon after that the man's wife became ill. She was sick all the time and no one could cure her, so they called in an

57

arbolario—someone who knows how to get rid of a spell. That witch had put a spell on the woman. So this man, he gave her all kinds of herbs and prayed a lot, and finally the woman recovered. He got rid of the witch's spell, I guess."

"Didn't people want to burn her or something?" I ask, thinking of the story "Los Tres Buyecitos."

"People don't do that anymore, 'jito, just in the story. Oh, in the old days, they said there were really, really bad witches, and they had to get rid of them. But this woman wasn't that bad, and anyway people don't burn witches anymore. That cuento "Los Tres Buyecitos" is just a story from a long time ago. . . ."

ONCE THERE LIVED A WOMAN who had three sons and a daughter. There came the day when the sons had to leave to seek their fortunes, and the mother and daughter were left by themselves.

A long time went by, and the sons did not return home to see their mother and sister. Finally, the mother died without ever seeing her sons again, and the daughter remained all alone. She felt lonely and after awhile she decided that she had nothing left to do but to go in search of her brothers.

The girl traveled for many days through the countryside but saw no one. Then one day she saw a little house in the middle of some fields of corn, squash, cabbage, and other vegetables. She was tired and hungry and hoped that she could find shelter there, but when she knocked on the door no one answered. Finally, she opened the door and went into the house. She was shocked at what she found.

"It looks like there is no woman here to clean this house! Everything is in disarray," thought the girl. She couldn't stand the mess and started putting everything in order and then began to make dinner.

In the evening she saw three young men walking down the road, and they were none other than her brothers! She could barely believe her eyes, especially when they came toward the house. "What luck!" she thought, but then she wondered if they would recognize her or welcome her to their home. To be safe, the girl hid in a back room.

When the three brothers walked through the door, they were surprised to find the house cleaned up, with dinner on the table. One man said to the other two, "I wonder who has done all this for us? I think there is someone hiding here." Then the brothers began searching all the rooms until finally they found the girl, but they didn't recognize her. After so many years she had grown up to be a beautiful young woman, and they began arguing about who should marry her.

But as they talked more with the girl the brothers began to notice little things about her that made them suspect her true identity. "Did you see how she seemed to know our names right away?" said the eldest brother. "And look, these tortillas are made just the way our mother made them!" After awhile, the brothers realized that the girl was their long-lost sister. She admitted it was true, and they were glad to see each other after so many years. "Now, we are all together again," they said, all happy.

Early the next morning the brothers prepared to leave for work again. But before they left, they warned their sister about the neighbor woman. "You must never go to the house next door, and you must always keep the door locked," they said, "for that neighbor woman is a witch who may do you harm."

Every day the men went to work early and came home late while the girl cleaned up the house and made dinner for them. Everything was going fine, and they were living happily together until one day the fire went out in the house. Without fire in the woodstove, the girl could not cook dinner, and she had no choice but to go ask the old witch next door for a piece of burning wood. So she put on her shawl and went down the road toward the witch's house.

As she approached the house, she met some boys walking down the road. "Where are you going, young lady?" asked one of them.

"I'm going to that house to get an ember to start my fire," answered the girl.

"That old woman is very wicked," said the boys. "She won't give you burning wood willingly. Be careful! And we'll also give you this advice: Look in the door before you go in, and if the witch has her eyes open you'll know she is asleep. But if her eyes are closed, then she's awake and you better not enter."

The girl went up to the witch's house and across the creaky old boards on the portal. When she peeked in the door, she saw that the witch had her eyes open. "What luck!" thought the girl. "The witch is asleep."

She entered the house quietly, grabbed a piece of burning wood from the corner fireplace, and placed it in her little bucket. Then she started running toward the door. But as she was leaving, she tripped on the doorstep, and the witch suddenly woke up. Right away the witch ran after the girl, but the girl was quick and reached her house before the witch could catch her, locking the door behind her.

The witch pounded on the door and shouted for the girl to let her in, but the girl didn't dare do so. When the witch realized that the girl wasn't going to let her in, she walked in a circle all around the house muttering something to herself and sprinkling a strange yellow liquid every once in a while. Wherever the potion fell, cabbages appeared from the ground. The girl watched from the window, then started a fire and lay down to take a nap. Running from the witch had made her tired.

That evening when the brothers returned from work they knocked and knocked on the door, but their sister didn't answer. They were extremely hungry, and when they saw the fresh cabbages growing all around the house they cut them up and ate them. No sooner had they all swallowed a few mouthfuls than they turned into little oxen.

When the girl finally woke up, she looked out the window and saw three oxen standing by the front door. Right away she suspected that the witch had transformed her brothers into these little animals. She was discouraged, but she vowed that from that day on she would take care of the three little oxen just as she had her brothers.

Every day the girl took the oxen down to a spring to drink water and then to pasture, where they would eat the grass. One day the king was riding down the road and saw the girl in the pasture with her oxen. The king thought she was very beautiful and immediately fell in love with her. He dismounted and approached the girl. They talked a little, and then he asked her to marry him.

"No," said the girl, "I can't marry you because I have my little oxen to take care of."

"I understand," said the king, "but don't worry. If you marry me, you can take them with you, and they will have the finest pasture in all this kingdom."

So the king and the girl were married, and she went to live with him in his castle. But the girl still kept caring for the oxen and was with them every day. One day when she took them to the spring to drink, she saw the old witch coming down the road to get water. Quickly, the girl climbed a tree so the witch would not see her.

The witch arrived at the spring and bent down to fill up her water jug. On the surface of the water, she saw the reflection of the girl above her in the tree. But thinking the image in the water was her own reflection, she said, "I am so beautiful! I shouldn't be hauling water! I'll break my water jug and go home."

Then she threw the jug down and turned to walk away, but when she turned around she saw the girl in the tree and realized that it wasn't herself that she had seen in the water but a reflection of the girl. Even though it was her own mistake, this made her angry with the girl. "Child, come down out of that tree so I can see you better," said the witch, trying to sound sweet.

But the girl knew that the witch didn't have good intentions. So she stayed in the tree until the witch grew tired of waiting and went on her way home, muttering under her breath that she would catch the girl some day.

Everything went back to normal, with the king and his new bride living happily in the castle while the three oxen enjoyed the royal pastures. After some time went by, the girl, now a young woman and a queen as well, had a baby. She cared for the child with much love, but she didn't forget her little oxen, and soon she was looking for someone to help her with the baby so she could take the oxen to water and pasture.

Now the witch saw an opportunity to make trouble. She fixed herself up in such a way that the queen would not recognize her, then she went to the castle and told the king that she wanted to be the queen's maid. The king agreed that she could take care of both the queen and the child.

The witch went into the queen's room, where she was sitting with her baby, and said, "My daughter, I am going to take care of you. Let me comb your hair so you will look beautiful for the king." Then while she was passing a comb through the queen's hair she stuck a pin in her scalp. Instantly, the queen turned into a white dove and flew out the window.

The witch smiled to herself as the dove flew away across the fields. Then she closed the curtains so the room would be dark, and she climbed into bed. When the king came in to sleep that night, she said that she was not feeling well and that she wanted to be alone in the dark room. The next day and night, she told him the same thing, and he let her be, thinking that she was tired from nursing the baby.

Time went by, and one day the king's servants were cutting wheat in the fields. A white dove flew by them, lit on a fence post, and then sang a song: "What does the king do with that Moorish woman? Does he sometimes sing and sometimes cry? And my little oxen, do they drink water from the spring and eat grass from the meadow?"

Right away the servants went to tell the king about the white dove that had talked and what she had said. The king told them to bring him the dove as soon as they could catch it. So the men went back to the fields and put some resin from a piñon tree on the fence post where the dove had landed. In a little while, the dove lit on the fence post as she had before. When the men went to grab the dove she couldn't fly away because her feet were stuck in the pitch, and they were able to lift her gently and take her to the king.

The king took the white dove in his hands and right away felt familiar with the bird. He started stroking the dove's head and talking to her softly. While he was touching her head, he felt a little lump, and when he pulled it, out came the pin that the witch had stuck in the queen's head. As soon as the pin came out, the dove turned back into the queen and was in the king's arms. Then the queen told the king that the woman lying in his bed was the old witch who had turned her into a dove and her brothers into oxen.

At hearing this the king ordered his servants to build a big bonfire with green firewood and to seize the old witch and throw her in it. The servants did as they were ordered, and while the witch was burning there was crackling and snapping like no one had ever heard before, until there was nothing left of the witch but a pile of ashes. As soon as she finished burning, the little oxen changed back into the three brothers. They went to live with the king and the queen in the castle, where they all lived happily ever after. ✦

The next thing I know, sunlight is flodding the kitchen next to our bedroom with yellow light and Grandma is frying potatoes for breakfast. I roll out of bed and Grandma says to me, "Buenos dias, my bueyecito!"

The Knight of the Feather

Today, Tío Isaías, or Uncle Ike as we know him better, invites me to go with him to the presa, *the diversion dam, and help him clean the Ortega* acequia. *It's early morning and the grasses and willows along the ditch are still wet from last night's thunderstorm.*

I've always loved being around the ditch, but I've never known about the work it takes to keep it flowing. Uncle Ike stops here and there and digs out debris, clears away rocks, hauls branches out of the flowing water. I help him when I can. We pass carefully tended orchards and fields and houses guarded by barking dogs and chickens. I want to go exploring these and the few crumbling old adobe buildings and several abandoned cars that are sinking into the ground, but Ike keeps me focused on the ditch and the work at hand as we make our way slowly upstream.

Eventually we reach the upper ditch in the foothills, where the landscape becomes wilder, more rugged. Steep slopes of broken rock rise up beside the ditch, and we have to cross deep ravines by walking along suspended culverts. It's difficult to balance on the slippery pipe, but my tío has confidence in me and doesn't even offer a hand. Once across the longest culvert, I feel that I've made a passage into an exclusive place.

The ditch near our house is lined mostly with small willows, wild plums, and a tangle of shrubs, but up here a verdant bosque *of giant cottonwood trees lines the* acequia. *The luxuriant underbrush is draped with vines of virgin's bower and Virginia creeper, and magpies swoop from tree to tree and a striped racer slithers along the ditch.*

This must be just what the Enchanted Garden was like for El Caballero de la Pluma—the hero of my favorite cuento. *As if to confirm my fantasy, I find a long, iri-*

descent magpie feather along the ditch and tuck it into the baseball hat that I'm wearing, imagining that I could be as clever and adventuresome as El Caballero de la Pluma.

We come to the end of the acequia, *where the Río Quemado rushes from a steep gorge in the foothills. It's like a gateway beckoning to the looming mountains beyond, and I want to keep going up the canyon. But we've reached our goal—the* presa, *a low dam of tree limbs and brush placed across the river, anchored with large river cobbles and patched with mud. Here Uncle Ike busies himself stopping leaks and coaxing more water into the* acequia.

"One time, when I was about your size," Uncle Ike says when he rests, "I came up here to help build the presa *in the spring. We worked all morning cutting* ramas *to pile up. We had to climb way up the hills, finding good trees and hauling them down. All of a sudden the* mayordomo *stopped us and yelled, 'Córreles, córreles!' and we all ran up the hillsides. We could barely climb, you know, it was so steep. Just imagine, 'jito. We were up there hanging on to* sabinos. *Then we heard a big roar, like thunder, and soon a wall of water and mud and rocks and logs, all mixed together, came roaring out of the canyon and washed away all our work from the morning. We were lucky it didn't get to us. And that wasn't the last time that the* presa *was washed away."*

As we make our way back down the acequia *and pass through the Enchanted Garden again, I'm wide-eyed and listening for the telltale roar of an approaching flood. That night, thoughts of the beautiful* bosque *and of the flood prompt me to ask Grandma to tell me the story of "El Caballero de la Pluma."*

"Oh, este muchacho, all he wants to hear is 'El Caballero de la Pluma,'" Grandma says. "Ya me cansé de esto. I'm tired of that one. And with that feather in your hat, you think you're El Caballero de la Pluma, or what? Bueno, mi hijito, I'll tell you again."

ONCE THERE WAS A MAN and his wife who had no family, and every day they asked God to send them a child. Just like the saying, "God may take his time in answering, but He doesn't forget," at last God granted them their wish by giving them a son.

When it came time to baptize the baby, they invited the neighbors to be the godparents. These neighbors were poor, and the only thing they had to take to their godson as a gift was a young colt.

When the boy was old enough, his parents told him that the colt was his own. Not having brothers or sisters to play with, he spent most of his time with the colt, and before long he passed more of his daytime hours with his colt than with his parents. Many nights he would even go and sleep with the horse. Since the boy was their only son, his parents were not happy about the state of affairs.

One night the boy heard his parents whispering together in the other room. He listened carefully and understood what they were saying.

"What we have to do is get rid of the colt," his father was telling his mother. "That's the only way we'll get them apart so we can spend time with our son. The first opportunity I get, I'll do it."

The boy got up early the next morning and told the colt about his parents' plan. "We will have to run away tonight," he said. "I would rather leave my parents than have them take you away."

The colt understood everything that the boy said because in those days animals had magical powers and could understand and speak people's language. He told the boy, "*Bueno,* we'll leave tonight, and I'll take you to a place where we'll be safe. We'll go to the castle of the king, and maybe he can give you some work. But I'm warning you. We'll be passing through dangerous places. You must stay on my back, and above all, do not touch anything that you see, no matter how beautiful it appears. If you do, bad luck will befall us!"

So they left that same night as soon as it was dark. After riding all night, the boy became sleepy. When he woke up early the next morning, just as the sun was rising, they were in a strange land that he had never seen before. They were passing through a lush garden, with flowers all around and lots of trees and a river. The trees seemed to glow like gold, and the water shone like silver. Birds of all colors flew through the trees singing songs. The boy was enchanted as if in a dream.

"This is the Enchanted Garden," said the colt. "Remember what I told you. Don't touch anything!"

The boy looked around him in awe. In spite of the colt's warning, he wanted so badly to touch the magical birds that when one flew close he couldn't resist the temptation to reach out for it. But the bird flew away before he could grasp it, and the boy was left with just one bright feather from its tail.

"You foolish boy!" said the colt. "Didn't I advise you not to touch anything, no matter how beautiful? Now, we will have bad luck for sure."

"Do you want me to throw the feather away?" asked the boy.

"No," answered his faithful colt. "If you did that, things would be worse."

So the boy tucked the feather in his hat, and from that day on everyone who saw him called him El Caballero de la Pluma, the Knight of the Feather.

They went on their way until they came to a wide river, swollen with floodwaters. To get to the king's castle, they had to cross the river, but it didn't seem that they could get through the deep, fast current. The boy was frightened, but the colt told him not to worry and to hang on tightly. They entered the water, and the colt swam boldly, with the boy clinging to his back. When they reached the other shore, they were no longer in the Enchanted Garden. Everything was plain as it had been before.

Finally, they came to the king's castle. The boy went in and asked the king if he could work for him. The king hired him, and after a while he saw that the boy was a good worker. In time, he favored El Caballero de la Pluma above his other workers, who had been there for much longer. So they became jealous of the boy and plotted to make him fall into disfavor with the king.

The workers devised a devious story and went to see the king. "Your Majesty," they told the king, "we know that your wife, the queen, lost her golden ring in the river long ago. El Caballero de la Pluma claims that he can get it back for you."

The king summoned the boy and said, "I understand that you can retrieve the ring that my wife lost in the river?"

"I never said that," the boy responded, remembering the fearful waters that he had crossed with the colt.

"Whether you said it or not, I don't care," replied the king. "I command you to do this today, and if you don't, fear for your life!"

El Caballero de la Pluma went and told his colt what had happened. "You know I can never get that ring from beneath the river," said the boy.

"This is the bad luck that I told you would happen," replied the colt. "It's all because you grabbed that feather when we were in the Enchanted Garden. But I have an idea for how you could do it." The horse talked quietly to the boy for a long time, and then the boy hurried off to town and bought a package of fine China paper.

When the boy came back to the castle, the king was waiting. "Well," said the king, "I am anxious for you to get the ring. We have missed it for many years." As he spoke, the townspeople gathered to watch, and the boy's fellow workmen whispered among themselves that this would be the end of El Caballero de la Pluma.

The boy went out behind the castle to the edge of the river. He opened the package of China paper and spread the sheets out, one by one, on the water. Slowly, the paper began to soak up the water. In a little while the river parted where the paper was laid, and El Caballero de la Pluma walked out and in no time found the queen's ring. The townspeople were amazed and cheered for the boy. The king, too, was surprised and pleased at what the boy had done—but the workers were angry. Muttering among themselves, they decided to make up another story.

The next day the workers went to the king again and said, "We know that you lost your marble throne in a shipwreck in the sea long ago. This Caballero de la Pluma claims that he can find it for you."

Again the king summoned El Caballero de la Pluma and told him of the rumors he had heard. The boy cried out that he could not perform this feat, for he had used up all the China paper in the town. But the king insisted, warning the boy, "I command you to do this today, and if you don't, fear for your life!"

When the boy went to the colt to bring him the news, the colt shook his head and stood quietly for a time. Finally he spoke: "Go to the town and gather all the horses you can find. They will come if you say that I sent you. When you come back, I'll tell you my plan."

As fast as he could, the boy went to town and whispered into the stalls of all the horses. They whinnied when he said the words that the colt had told him, and they jumped the fences of their corrals to follow him. When he returned to the castle, he had thousands and thousands of horses with him.

The colt made neighing and whinnying noises as the horses passed him, and they all lined up beside the sea. The boy didn't know what to do, but his faithful colt said to him, "I have told the horses what to do. All you have to do is slap your whip against the castle wall three times, and the way to get the throne will become clear."

The boy stood before the king and the assembled people who had come from all over the kingdom, for they had heard of the amazing feat that El Caballero de la Pluma had done before. The king said, "Well, can you find my marble throne beneath those waves?"

"I can," said the boy, and he slapped the castle wall three times with his leather whip. All at once the horses reared and plunged into the sea, and as they entered they made such a splash that all the water rushed away. There on the bottom of the ocean, El Caballero de la Pluma spied the marble throne, half buried in mud. Quickly he jumped on his colt and rode out.

As he neared the throne, the waters of the sea began to close in again. He had little time, but he threw a rope around the throne and the colt pulled hard. Finally, the throne came up from the mud, and they raced to the shore, just as the sea came crashing back, flooding the path they had taken.

The king was so happy to have his throne back that he immediately made El Caballero de la Pluma the boss of all his workers. And even though they had been envious of him before, the workers now admired El Caballero de la Pluma and were glad to work for him.

El Caballero de la Pluma was grateful to his colt and loved him more than ever, but he hadn't forgotten his parents. So he asked the king's permission to bring them to the castle, which the king granted gladly. Then he rode off on his colt, back across the wild river and through the Enchanted Garden. This time he was careful to leave well enough alone. He didn't try to grab the beautiful birds but instead only admired them from horseback. He marveled at the glowing trees without wanting to take them with him.

When he came to his old home, his parents wept with joy at seeing him. "We're so sorry that we planned to get rid of that colt," they said. "We only wanted to spend more time with you." El Caballero de la Pluma told them that he forgave them and told of his adventures with the colt. His parents were astonished at what the horse could do and said, "We never knew that your colt had magical powers." Then El Caballero de la Pluma and his parents saddled up their horses and rode back to the castle, where the king gave them big rooms, fine clothing, and all the food they could eat. There El Caballero de la Pluma, his parents, and the fine colt lived for the rest of their lives. ✦

María Bernarda

The screened-in porch on the east side of the house is a cool refuge from the summer sun. It's late one afternoon and the heat has become too much for both Grandma and me. We go out to the porch and Grandma says, "Vamos a comer sandía." She carries a ripe watermelon from the kitchen and begins carving off slabs with a kitchen knife. We delight in the cool, sweet flesh of the melon while flies drone lazily on the screens around us.

Grandma is wearing a broad-brimmed straw hat tied beneath her chin with a ribbon of cloth. She wears a simple cotton dress that she sewed herself many years ago and that she will wear for many more years. She talks between mouthfuls of watermelon, describing the days when her father grew melons much sweeter than these and how he would take them to Santa Fe to sell in the plaza. She points with the knife across the road, indicating where the melons grew.

"And we used to take melons to Santa Clara Pueblo on feast day," she says, "and the family would sit around the wagon in the shade of the cottonwoods eating those big, sweet melons. But crossing the Santa Cruz River to get there, oh that was scary. Sometimes even the horses had a time getting across because there was no bridge, you know. And I would close my eyes and pray every time we crossed, like that girl in the story, María Bernarda. . . ."

ONCE THERE WAS A YOUNG GIRL named María Bernarda. She had a little mule that had grown up with her since she was a child. María and the mule were so close that they could talk to each other, just like people. Long ago many people could do this because animals had magical powers.

Bueno, pues, María, she was beautiful but also very arrogant, you know, too good for everyone else. Many young men came to ask for her hand in marriage, but she didn't want to marry any of them. She would turn her head and say, "I'm not going to marry until the one who asks me has gold teeth and a silver beard."

Well, the devil found out about what María was saying, and he fixed himself up with gold teeth and a silver beard and went to propose to her. When María saw his gold teeth and silver beard, she told him right away that she would marry him. She thought he was just the man she had been waiting for! *Qué tonta, no?*

María went to tell the mule that she had finally met the man she would marry. But instead of being happy, the mule was upset because he knew right away that the man with the gold teeth and silver beard was evil. She told María, "*Ahh, qué muchita está!* The one that has asked you to be his wife is none other than the devil!"

"*Es cierto?* Don't tell me that! What am I going to do now?" asked María, very agitated.

"Well, tell him that you won't leave your house without your little mule, and always wear your scapular. I will warn you of his tricks, and the scapular will keep him away from you," the mule told her.

"*Bueno, amigita,*" said María. "I won't remove my scapular, and I'll stay close to you."

The devil mounted his horse and María her mule, and they set off for the devil's home far away. They had only traveled a little while when they came to a big, red river of blood. They stopped and looked at the terrible flood. María didn't know how they would get across.

"Don't worry," said the mule to María. "Just tell the devil that you'll go first, and everything will be fine—but remember to hold onto me and your scapular!"

So María told the devil that she would go first, and holding one hand on her scapular and the other on the mule they entered the river. Just then the river parted to let them pass, and they didn't get a drop of blood on them.

Then the devil followed them, but when he began to cross, the river of blood closed in on him, and he and his horse arrived at the other shore drenched with blood. The devil's horse shook and stamped to get the blood off, and the devil frowned with his ugly face. María saw that his gold teeth and silver beard didn't shine so brightly anymore.

After a while they went on their way down the road. But soon they came to another river—a river of spears. Once again the mule and María went first, and the river of spears parted and let them pass. But when the devil began to cross, the spears came together all at once and pierced his body. He shrieked and his horse reared, but they made it to the other side. The devil scowled at María very meanly but didn't say a word.

They traveled onward toward the devil's house, but soon they came to yet another river. This river was pure fire, and it nearly burned them just to get close to it. María was frightened, but, trusting her old friend the mule, she closed her eyes and held onto her scapular while the mule stepped into the flames. All at once the flames parted, making a path for the mule and María, and they passed through without getting burned. Then came the devil's turn. He smiled because he was used to heat and fire, you know, and didn't think he could be burned. But when he started across, the flames closed in on him, and although he made it to the other side he was badly burned. He was too angry to speak, and his gold teeth and silver beard were black from the smoke.

The travelers were getting near the devil's house, and María became afraid. If they reached his home, she would have to live with the devil there for the rest of her days! She thought about all the times she had turned away fine young men. "I had many chances to marry, but I believed I was too good for all of them," she thought. "If I get out of this, I never want to marry at all!"

The riders continued until they came to the last river before the devil's house. There before them was a wide river of sharp knives. They could see the devil's house on the other side. For a final time, the mule and María entered first, María with her eyes closed and her hand tightly wrapped around her scapular. Suddenly the knives pulled back and let them pass. Quickly the devil entered the opening, following closely to avoid the blades. But as soon as the devil's horse stepped in, the knives came clashing together and cut the devil all over his body. At this, the devil could take no more and fell over dead.

"Holy Mary has been watching over you!" the mule cried. "Now we will continue with our journey to see what fortune awaits us." María was happy to be free of the devil, but she vowed never to agree to marriage again. Then she and the mule set off at a trot, not knowing what was ahead.

After a while they came to a pasture where some shepherds were watching over their sheep, and María had an idea for a way to avoid any future marriage proposals. She asked the shepherds for men's clothing, and they offered her some old worn-out clothes full of holes. María put them on, climbed on the mule, and they continued down the road.

In a few days they came to the king's castle. María wanted very much to live there because it was such a beautiful place, so she told the king that her name was Bernardo and that she was in search of work. The king looked her over and offered her a job.

Now, this king had a son who was always melancholy and would never say a word. All day he would sit on the balcony of the castle, watching people go by. One day he saw María Bernarda, whom everyone called Bernardo, passing below. He called out to her, "Look at that lad!"

Everyone was shocked that the prince had spoken. The king and queen were so happy that they called to "Bernardo" and said that from that moment on they wanted Bernardo to be the prince's constant companion. So every day María chatted with the prince, and they took walks around the castle grounds. Day by day the prince felt happier and more attached to "Bernardo." One afternoon he told the queen, "You know what? I have a feeling that my friend Bernardo's eyes really belong to Bernardita."

"No! Why do you say that?" said the queen. "He's a man, my son. But to find out for sure, tomorrow I will tell one of the servants to take him to the garden. If he likes the flowers, it's a sign that Bernardo is Bernardita."

The mule was listening to everything that the prince and queen said, and she went to María and told her about their plans.

The following day the servant told María, "Let's go visit the flower garden."

"Oh, no thank you," said María. "I'm not interested in flowers. Only women are interested in those things."

The servant rushed back to the queen's quarters. "How did Bernardo like the flowers?" asked the queen.

"He didn't even want to go to the garden," said the servant. "He said he wasn't interested in flowers."

The queen called for the prince and told him, "You see? Your friend Bernardo is a man. He doesn't like flowers."

"Oh, no," answered the prince. "It still seems to me that those dark eyes of Bernardo belong to Bernardita. I just know it."

"Bueno," said the queen. "If you're so sure, tomorrow you ask him to go horseback riding. Give him the wildest horse and see if he can manage it. If he can, we'll know he's a man, but if he can't we'll know it's Bernardita."

The mule was standing below the queen's window eating some grass and heard their conversation. She went to María and told her what they had said.

"What will I do this time, my friend?" asked María. "I only know how to ride you!"

"Listen," said the mule, "just don't use the saddle that they give you. Use mine instead, and you'll ride as if you were riding me."

The next day they went to the corral, and a servant lassoed a wild-eyed stallion that snorted and bucked as the prince went to put on the saddle. "Bernardo, my friend, this will be your mount," he said.

"That's fine," María said. "But I only ride with my own saddle."

"All right," said the prince. And he put the little mule's saddle on the bucking horse. Once María settled onto the saddle, however, the horse became calm. They went out to the fields, and María was as good a rider as the prince. He complimented María on her skill but still was not convinced that his friend was a man. Afterwards he went to the castle and told the queen about their ride.

"Well, you are hard to persuade," the queen said. "But I have one more test. Tonight we will send out one of the servants to see Bernardo when he is sleeping. Without his hat, we'll know if he's a man or a woman."

This time the mule was in the corral eating hay and didn't hear the conversation between the queen and the prince. She and María thought that they had finally proven to the prince that she was a man. But that night when she was sound asleep the servant crept to her room to see "Bernardo" while he was sleeping. He took one look and saw that "Bernardo" had hair that came all the way down to his waist! The servant ran immediately to the queen and told her what he had seen.

In the morning the queen said to the prince, "I guess you were right, my son. Go and tell your friend that we know her secret. Perhaps she will tell us who she really is."

As soon as he heard the news, the prince went to María and said, "We have discovered your secret, Bernardo! I always suspected that you were a woman, and I fell in love with you. Now I know that those dark eyes belong to Bernardita, and the only thing I want to be happy in this world is for you to be my princess."

Shocked that she had been found out, María looked at her mule. The mule put her ears back and told her, "I guess we couldn't keep our secret forever. I think you should marry this fine young man."

So María consented to marry the prince—but only if she could bring her mule to live with them. The prince agreed, and thereafter the prince, María Bernarda, and her little mule lived happily together. ⬧

The Little Shepherd

The best place to watch the sunset is from the top of the fuerte *behind Grandma's house. As with all the old buildings in Chimayó, it takes me a long time to understand the original use of this building, now falling into ruin. To me, it has a function as it is—a place to sit on a high vantage and watch the sun go down. It's also another place to play around and explore odds and ends abandoned long ago.*

Grandma uses this word fuerte *in many ways, and I come to understand that it means "strong"—a strong building. She uses the word also to describe the small log buildings that her father erected up at Llano Abeyta, near Truchas, where he maintained wheat fields. She would stay in the* fuerte *at Llano Abeyta to help out during the wheat harvest, cooking over an open fire in the* fuerte *while the men cut wheat all day and into the night.*

I sit up on the fuerte *and watch the sun set on summer evenings when the air is cooling off. The taste of red chile lingers like a warm glow that matches the sky. The gentle lines of the Jemez Mountains rest on the western horizon beneath a blaze of orange and red that grows richer and deeper every moment, while to the east the twilight darkens the foothills and Venus appears. A warm summer breeze stirs the leaves of the giant poplar, locust, and cottonwood trees along the ditch.*

The gaps between the logs of the fuerte *were never filled, and the collection of junk inside is exposed to the weather and has rusted and become useless. There are rolls of chicken wire, leak-ridden watering troughs, buckets and barrels, and rolls of baling wire. Broken bottles and pieces of damaged tools. Battered chamber pots. Old tin signs and stacks of rotting scavenged lumber.*

Grandma comes out to look for me, sees me atop the fuerte *and signals me down. "Qué tienes, 'jito. Estás loco, o qué? Get down from there! Vente p'acá!"*

I jump down from the roof and go to the house. "Why do you play around that old place?" Grandma asks me. "It's dangerous there."

The fuerte *is where her father used to keep his animals. "You see there, where all those trees are sprouting up. That's where the pigpen was. Haven't you noticed it still stinks like pigs there? And we had a horse, too, when my father was alive. He called him Dandy and he used to keep hay for him in the* fuerte, *and there was a little corral out back. When Dandy died, my father cried a lot. He loved that horse—it was a big white horse, and it would come to him when he called. And it pulled his plows for many, many years.*

"The chickens, they lived on the east side of the fuerte *in that little yard, and at night we'd lock them inside that little adobe room there. I used to love to go get the eggs every morning, and I'd watch those chickens and try to understand them! I'd think of the story of 'El Pastorcillo' and wonder what those chickens and the rooster were saying."*

ONCE THERE WAS A YOUNG MAN who was a shepherd. Every day he would go to the mountains to watch over his sheep. He kept a little fire going to cook his meals and to warm himself at night. He was very content there in the mountains with his sheep.

One day he built his fire too close to some dry branches, and they caught fire. The shepherd ran back to his camp and started beating the fire with his blanket to try and put it out. Near a burning log he saw a little snake trying to escape from the flames. Feeling sorry for the trapped animal, the shepherd grabbed a stick and pulled it out of the fire.

The little snake was grateful to the shepherd for saving her life, and she told El Pastorcillo, "Because you have been so kind to me, I'm going to take you to see my father, the big snake. He is very powerful, and I want you to ask him for a gift. But I'm warning you: Don't ask him for riches or anything like that because such a request will anger him, and he may kill you. Just tell him that you want to understand the language of the animals. He will not agree right away, for this is much to ask, but keep telling him that is all you desire."

They walked through the mountains until they came to where the father snake lived. He was curled up beneath a big, round rock. When he saw the man approaching with his daughter, he seemed agitated and nervously stuck out his tongue. The man and the little snake approached the big snake and told him what the shepherd had done for her. "Because he saved my life," she said, "I want you to grant him a wish."

The big snake said, "All right then, what is your wish?"

"I want to understand the language of the animals," said the shepherd.

The big snake drew back into a coil, frowned, and responded, "Ask for something else instead."

"No," answered the shepherd. "That is all I want."

"All right then," said the big snake in a little while, "I will grant you this wish, but I'm warning you: The day you tell another person that you understand the language of the animals you will die."

The shepherd returned to watch over his sheep and sat under a pine tree. He was wondering what good it would be to understand the language of the animals when two crows landed above him on the tree. When they began to call out to each other like "crows do—"caw, caw!—the shepherd could understand what they were saying!

One crow said to the other, "What if this poor shepherd knew that beneath this very tree there is a buried treasure?"

"Well, he would become a wealthy man," answered the other. "But he will never know!" And the two crows began to laugh as they flew away—"Caw, caw, caw."

The shepherd wasted no time. Right away he grabbed a shovel and began digging beneath the tree until he found a big jar full of gold coins. With all that money, he became a rich man and didn't have to tend sheep for a living anymore. "Now, I will have a house and marry a good wife," said the shepherd.

So the shepherd left the mountains and built a house in the valley. Then he married a beautiful girl, and the two made their home together. At first the shepherd missed his sheep and the mountains, but he soon became content with his wife and what little livestock he kept in the barn.

One day the shepherd and his wife went horseback riding. He rode a stallion, and his wife rode a mare. After they were riding for a little while, the stallion turned his head back toward the mare and whinnied. Because the man knew the language of the animals, he understood what the stallion said to the mare: "Go faster, you lazy thing!"

The mare perked up her ears and rolled back her lip, letting out a snicker. The woman paid the noise no mind, but the man understood what the mare was saying: "Sure, that's easy for you to say. You are carrying only one rider, and I am carrying two! How do you expect me to keep up with you?"

When the man heard what the mare told the stallion, he burst out laughing and kept laughing as they rode down the road. "My wife is pregnant, and we will have a child!" he thought.

His wife looked at him strangely and asked, "Why are you laughing so much?"

"Oh, just because I feel like laughing," answered her husband.

"Tell me why you are laughing!" demanded the woman.

"Oh, I can't tell you," answered the man.

"You have to tell me why you are laughing!" the woman insisted. "What were you thinking about that made you laugh? Do I look funny?"

After a while the man grew tired, and they turned around and headed back toward their house. All the way home the wife pestered her husband. He tried telling her everything he could to make her lose interest in what he was thinking, but she became angrier and angrier and demanded that he tell her.

When they reached the house, the wife still kept insisting he tell her what was so funny. She bothered him so much that finally the poor man decided he would have to tell her why he was laughing just so she would leave him in peace. The shepherd remembered well what the father snake had told him, but in order to explain to his wife, he would have to tell her that he understood the language of the animals. Once he did that he would die.

The following day the man rose early and started making his coffin. In the afternoon he finished and sat outside to rest. He was sad because he knew what was going to happen to him. Watching the animals in the barnyard, he missed his days of peace and freedom in the mountains. Now he wished he had never found that snake in the fire!

The dog was lying down by his master and said to the rooster, who was crowing loudly nearby, "Why are you so happy? Don't you know that our master is going to die?"

"Let him die," said the rooster. "Why is he so foolish? When I find a kernel of corn, I don't call the hens! I eat the kernel before they get there."

The man was listening and understood what the

rooster was saying. He thought, "What the rooster is saying is true. I am an idiot! I don't have to tell my wife everything!"

Right away the man went back to the house and found his wife in the kitchen. "Are you going to tell me what is so funny now?" she asked.

"No, I'm not," said the shepherd. "You should stop pestering me, and we can live in peace!" He locked his wife in a room and told her he was going to leave her alone there until she stopped tormenting him. The woman pleaded with the man, but after a while she saw that her husband was not going to give in to her. So she promised him that she would never again mention anything about his laughter or what he was thinking.

In a few months the woman's belly began to swell, and soon she had a baby boy. The man chuckled to himself, for he had known all along that she was pregnant. As he held the baby on his knee, he thought, "If only I could understand the language of babies."

Nobody ever learned that man's secret. Many times the animals helped him, and he and his wife and child lived a long and happy life. ✤

A few years after I graduate from high school and leave New Mexico, I come home to find the fuerte *completely gone. Not a trace of the building or any of the things once inside it remain. I rush into Grandma's house and ask what happened.*

"Oh, I asked a man down the road to clean it up for me," she said. "Qué suave, no? He cleaned it really nice, didn't he? They brought in a bulldozer and knocked that place down. It was old and junky, and it looked like some real poor, ignorant people lived there who didn't care about the place."

Now, where the fuerte *once stood, a thick grove of trees is growing amid the cactus, nurtured by the deep layers of detritus around the pigpen and chicken coop.*

Foolish John

"Let's go to the arbolitos," Grandma says as she grabs some empty lard cans and strides out into the already hot sun of midmorning. I follow her out the driveway and down the road past the weaving shop, where we can hear an A.M. radio playing and the rhythm of the looms pounding.

We continue down the dirt road to the highway, which Grandma still calls the new road even though it's been there for many years. "Antes, you know, they used to have the carreras here—the horse races for día del Santiago," Grandma says. "Over there by the arroyo they would race and try and steal the rooster from each other. We'd walk over here up the arroyo, before they put fences there and before the new road was in. Oh, your grandpa—or I guess he was your visabuelo, que no?—his land went all the way to the arroyo, but now it's cut in half and they put that fence up so we can't get to the land from the arroyo anymore.

"And over there, behind Davíd's house, there used to be a cemetery there and we could go there, but now it's fenced, too, and I don't know what happened to those graves. They only had wooden crosses, you know, but one of my sisters was buried there, I think, when I was just a little girl."

I'm barely paying attention to the story that Grandma is telling. I'm lost in the spell of the day, smelling the good smells of earth and dry grass and watching for snakes and lizards. But I hear her, as I will hear many times, as she tells the history of this place.

We stop to let a car go by. Grandma squints from beneath the simple cotton bonnet that she made and now wears every time we go out into the sun. She peers out and we cross the pavement of the new road and come to a barbed-wire fence. Grandma hitches up her dress, and I'm surprised at her agility as, in one motion, she *parts the wires, swings one leg through, then one arm and her upper body, the lard cans swinging from her hand. She smiles at me, saying, "A little fence can't stop an old Chimayosa like me!" Then she turns and lifts the wire for me with her other hand, and we walk across the empty field to another fence. Again, we duck through and then we're in the* arbolitos, *a tiny cluster of aging fruit trees along the Ortega* acequia.

I look across the ditch, which is lined with wild plums and roses, to the Cañada Ancha arroyo, where the sand shines brilliantly behind the shaded greenery. This is new territory for me, and I feel vulnerable and excited. We're on the other side of the highway, the road I'm forbidden to cross, and the arroyo beckons like a gateway to new places and to the mysterious badlands beyond.

This tiny orchard we've come to visit is the only patch of agricultural land left to Grandma, the last remnants in my family of my great-grandpa's vast holdings that included several large orchards, fields of chile, corn, beans, squash, and melons, as well as acres of land on the llano *for growing wheat. Now, all we have is the* arboli-tos, *and the apricot, plum, and apple trees are dry and full of dead branches. Still, the plums are loaded with fruit. Grandma talks about how much she loved to come here for the* ciruelas *when she was a child. I jump into the tree to reach the high branch-es for her, and she calls to me, "Cuídate, 'jito!" but she's glad that I can reach the plums higher up.*

"You look like Juan Tonto up there!" Grandma says.

"Ya mero, Grandma, ya mero!" I reply, and she laughs out loud.

ONCE UPON A TIME there lived a woman who had a son named Juan. Everyone called him Juan Tonto because he was always doing foolish things. One morning while Juan was still snoring, his mother told him, "Juan, get up and see if the fire is still going."

Juan called to the cat and touched it. "Yes, the fire is still going, Mama. The cat is hot."

The poor woman wanted Juan to get up and do something to earn a living. She told him, "Juan, get up and see if it rained last night."

But instead Juan just called the dog and touched him, telling his mother, "Yes, it rained last night, Mama. The dog is still wet."

Trying again to rouse him, his mother then said,

"You know what, Juan? Your neighbor already got up, and he found a bag full of money."

"The person who lost the money got up earlier," answered Juan.

"God help me, Juan," said his mother finally. "I have to go look for work to earn money so we can buy food. You are so lazy that if I wait until you do something we will die of hunger. Take care of the baby while I'm gone."

"*Bueno*, Mama, go ahead and find work," Juan answered, still too lazy to get up.

Soon after Juan's mother left, the baby started crying. But Juan was even too lazy to get out of bed and pick him up, so the baby kept crying. Finally,

Juan yelled across the room, "Oh, *cállate!*" and threw one of his shoes at the baby's bed. The baby became quiet, and Juan thought, "I taught that baby something now. Why doesn't my mother show him who's boss like that?"

Later in the day Juan's mother returned home and asked him, "How is the baby?"

"Oh," said Juan, "he cried for a while, but I taught him a lesson, and he has slept all day."

The mother went to see the baby and noticed that he had been knocked unconscious by Juan's big shoe. There was a huge bruise on the poor baby's head. "What did you do to my baby?" exclaimed the mother. "I'll have to give my baby to his grandmother. Now I am leaving to find work, and I'm never coming back! You stay here and watch the door so that no one will come in!"

The poor woman left, and Juan Tonto was all alone. "What am I going to do without my mother?" thought Juan. After a while he couldn't stand to be there without his mother, so he removed the door, put it on his back, and went down the road after her. It was late in the day when he caught up with her.

"Juan, why did you follow me? And what are you doing with that door on your back?" Juan's mother cried, unable to believe that he had followed her.

"Well, Mama, what was I going to do alone? And you told me to watch the door, so I brought it with me," answered Juan.

"*Dios mío,* I have no choice but to suffer whatever is my lot," said the poor mother.

They had walked a long way when they saw in the distance many men on horseback. "What are all those men doing so far from everything?" Juan's mother wondered. "They must be up to no good, Juan. Let's climb that tree so they won't notice us."

Juan's mother climbed the tree, and Juan followed her with the door on his back. No sooner had they climbed up when the gang of men arrived. They were thieves who had with them many sacks of money. They started to make dinner right under the tree where Juan and his mother were hiding.

Then the men began to talk about all the robberies they had been involved in and how much money they had stashed away in the little house nearby. While they were chatting, Juan and his mother were listening to everything they said.

After a while Juan whispered to his mother, "Mama, I have to pee!"

"Oh, Juan, *aguanta!* Just hold it!" whispered his mother.

In a few minutes, Juan repeated, "Mama, I'm about to pee!"

"*Aguanta,* hold it, Juan, hold it!" his mother whispered again sternly.

But Juan couldn't hold it, so his mother took off her boot and said, "Use this!" Juan tried to pee in the boot, but his aim wasn't too good, and some droplets spilled down from the tree onto the robbers below. One of the robbers looked up in the tree as he brushed off his shirt, and Juan and his mother thought for sure they had been found out. "Those dirty birds!" the thief said. He didn't see Juan and his mother through the branches.

Juan's mother was relieved, but in just a few minutes Juan whispered to her, "Mama, Mama, I have to caca!"

"Don't tell me this, Juan! They'll find us for sure, and they'll kill us. Hold it!"

"I can't, Mama," said Juan.

"*Aguanta!* Hold it, Juan, just hold it a little while!"

"I can't, Mama!"

"*Bueno,* Juan, be quiet and take my boot!" Juan's mother said, and Juan tried to go in the boot, but his aim wasn't too good, and some fell down through the branches and hit the robbers below. "Ahh, those dirty birds!" said one of the thieves, looking up into the tree. "Maybe I should shoot them so they'll stop making droppings on us."

The men went back to smoking and talking, and Juan and his mother felt they were safe. But they wondered how long they'd have to stay up in the tree.

After a while Juan leaned over to his mother and whispered, "Mama, I can't hold this door anymore!"

"For the love of God, Juan, *aguanta!* Just hold it!" said his mother.

"I can't hold it, Mama!" Juan said, and before she could speak he dropped the door.

The door went tumbling down through the tree branches, breaking many as it fell. The robbers were surprised and looked up to see what all the racket was. One of the gang saw Juan and his mother and began to shout to the others, but just as he was about to speak the door struck him on the mouth and split his tongue in two.

The robber wanted to shout to the others that there were two people in the tree, but instead of words just nonsense came out of his mouth, and he said, "Biliabila bilia brilit!" The other thieves were terrified by their companion's behavior, and they all took off running, with the injured man shouting gibberish after them. They left all their horses tied up beneath the tree with the sacks of money on their backs.

Juan and his mother waited a while to see if the thieves would return. Then when they were sure that they were not coming back, they came down from the tree, taking the sacks of money that the thieves had left behind with them.

The next morning Juan rose early and went to find men to help him build a house. Now that he had so much money, his laziness and stupidity seemed to have vanished. As soon as the people saw Juan building a house, they told the king, for no one could believe that Juan Tonto could have enough money or smarts to build a house. The people told the king that this house would be more beautiful than his castle.

"But how can that be?" exclaimed the king. "Juan Tonto can't possibly have that much money." The king immediately ordered two of his servants to get Juan. When Juan appeared before the king, the king asked him, "Tell me, Juan, how did you get so rich overnight? Aren't you the one they used to call Juan Tonto?"

"I'm the one, and I got it by stealing, Your Majesty," said Juan.

"So, you are a thief!" said the king.

"And an expert thief at that," answered Juan.

"All right," said the king. "Tonight I want you to steal the sheet on which I sleep. If you can do that, I will not only believe that you are an expert thief but I will also give you half of all my money. If you can't then fear for your life!"

Juan went home and made a life-sized doll resembling himself and attached a cord to it. When night came, he went to the castle and set the doll near the window where the king and queen slept. They were wide awake, waiting for Juan to come and steal the sheet. When the king saw the figure near the window, he said to the queen, "There's Juan! I'm going to chase him away."

The king went out, and Juan pulled the cord attached to the doll. The doll started running, and the king went running after it. Then Juan came into the dark room and told the queen, "Hide the sheet in the trunk that is out in the hall so Juan won't find it."

Soon after, the king returned to his room and told the queen, "I chased that Juan Tonto away!"

"Didn't you come in a while ago and ask me to hide the sheet in the trunk?" asked the queen.

"That wasn't me," answered the king. "Juan has pulled one over on us!"

The next day Juan went to return the sheet to the king, and the king said, "This robbery doesn't count. You played a trick on me. Tonight, I want you to steal the bread from the oven."

So Juan went and bought a priest's vestment, a prayer book, a bag, and a gallon of wine. That night the king had many soldiers watching the bread in the oven. But when they saw Juan coming toward them, they said, "Look, it is only a priest praying. Let him pass."

Juan walked over and asked them what they were doing.

"We are watching over the bread that is in the

oven because Juan Tonto is going to try to steal it," they answered.

"Oh, that Juan Tonto, what will he do next? Would you like a drink of wine?" asked Juan.

They accepted the offer, and quick as a wink they drank the gallon of wine and went to sleep because they were so drunk. Then Juan took the bread out of the oven, put it in his bag, and went home.

The following day Juan took the bread back to the king. The king said to him, "Last night doesn't count because my watchmen got drunk. It was easy for you to steal the bread. In order for me to believe that you are an expert at robbery, tonight you must steal all the money I possess. If you can accomplish this, I will have no doubts that you are a true thief."

This time Juan left to buy an angel costume and a rope. Later that night he went to the king's chapel, climbed the tower, and started ringing the bell. The king told the queen, "I'm going to see who is ringing the bell at this hour of the night!"

When the king arrived at the chapel, he looked up and saw an angel in the bell tower. He went closer to see if it truly was an angel, and when he was close enough, Juan said to him, "I am an angel who has come to take you to heaven. God wants your body and soul so that you won't suffer in this world. Do you want to go?"

"Yes, yes, I am a good Christian, and I am ready to go to heaven," the king replied enthusiastically.

"All right," said Juan. "But before I can take you with me to heaven, you have to put all your money in one place so the poor will make use of it."

"Whatever you say," answered the king, and he left hurriedly for the castle. When he returned to the chapel, Juan asked him, "Did you put all your money in one place?"

"Yes," answered the king. "I left it all behind the castle door. I am ready to go."

"All right," said the "angel" Juan. "Hold onto this rope and close your eyes."

Juan started pulling the rope, and when the king was high up in the air he let go of it. The king fell down with such force that he was knocked unconscious. Juan climbed down from the tower, took the king in his arms, and carried him to the chicken coop. Then he went straight to the place where the king had put all his money and took it home.

The next day at dawn, when the roosters were crowing, the king slowly woke up. He looked around at all the chickens and said to himself, "I guess there are roosters in heaven, too!"

After a while a servant went to feed the chickens and found the king lying among them more dead than alive. She helped him up and took him to the castle.

Later in the day Juan came to return the money. "Now I really believe you are an expert thief!" exclaimed the king. "Not only will I give you half my money but I will also give you my daughter in marriage."

Juan didn't accept the money since he had plenty of his own. He did, however, accept the offer to marry the king's daughter. Soon they were married, and they lived happily ever after. ✣

The Lion, the Tiger, and Don José, the Bear

Tía Juanita shares none of Grandma's penchant for storytelling. In fact, she is reticent to the point of seeming cold and distant. She comes to stay at Grandpa Reyes's old house from time to time across the road from Grandma's. Tía Juanita inherited the house from her father because, as the only unmarried daughter, she took care of Reyes in his declining years.

Underneath Tía Juanita's stoic exterior, I sense a warm heart that longs for human contact, and sometimes it shines through. She gives me candies and lets me bang on the piano in the sala *that Reyes bought for his five daughters. I like to visit Tía Juanita because it affords me the opportunity to go into the ancient home of Grandpa Reyes.*

The house always smells musty because no one lives there except when Tía Juanita visits. The sala *was built below ground level, so entering you walk down a few steps. The earthen berm along the north wall keeps the house cool. This is the room where Reyes displayed his blankets for sale to tourists who began coming to Chimayó when the new road was built in the late 1930s. Grandma tells me that he used to have hundreds of blankets stacked on the* bancos *along the walls.*

Tía Juanita seldom lets me go beyond the sala, *but I do get a peak now and then into the room where Grandma was born. It's dark and cold; the fireplace in the corner hasn't been lit in decades. This is also the room where Reyes's wife, Genoveva, died in childbirth, leaving Reyes with five daughters to raise.*

Tía Juanita doesn't tell us cuentos, but she has two of them written down, and one day she offers to read one to Grandma and me. The idea of a written cuento seems strange, but when she tells me the story is about a boy whose friends are a lion, a tiger, and a bear my interest is piqued. Such animals are mythical creatures in Chimayó, but I've heard true stories about them from my cousins in Cundiyó, just over the hills to the east. There, encounters with real mountain lions and black bears are not uncommon.

The Cundiyosos are legendary mountain people, accustomed to a different kind of life than ours in the valley. They grow the same crops and weave blankets in the same style, but the air in Cundiyó is always noticeably cooler, snow lingers on the ground later into the spring, and the looming presence of the mountains is immediate and pressing. The cold mountain streams make their first exit from forested canyons into irrigated farmland at Cundiyó, creating a constant clamor.

Occasionally we drive the twisty, narrow, unpaved road to Cundiyó to visit Grandma's cousins Pulas and Noberto. They have earned reputations as great hunters, and Noberto served as a game warden for a time. The two brothers bring home fresh elk or deer meat every year, and on many occasions they have shot mountain lions, which are a menace to the village because they kill sheep, cattle, horses, and goats. Black bears don't go after livestock but they damage the orchard trees and steal fruit.

Grandma and I sit together in the old rocking chair in the sala, *and Tía Juanita begins reading her story about some children who I believe must have lived in Cundiyó.*

ONCE THERE WAS A MAN AND WOMAN who lived in the mountains with a daughter and a son. The boy and girl were very young when their parents died, leaving the two alone in the house. But they learned to get along by themselves, and one day the girl said to the boy, "Brother, now that we're all alone let's promise that neither one of us will ever marry."

"All right," said the boy, and the two of them agreed never to marry.

The boy had a lion, a tiger, and a bear named Don José that he had raised since he was a child. These animals were well trained to do everything that their master ordered. To take care of his little sister and keep food on the table, the boy would

often hunt for game in the mountains with the help of his animal friends.

One day the boy went out with his little animals to hunt, and while he was gone a giant came to the house and went in to find the girl all alone. The giant fell in love with the girl, and the girl fell in love with the giant. But when the giant asked her if she would marry him, the girl said, "My brother and I have promised never to marry."

The giant told her that he could kill her brother if she would let him marry her. The girl answered, "All right, but I don't know which direction my brother goes when he hunts every day."

"Oh," said the giant, "this evening when he comes

home, ask him which way he's going tomorrow."

The girl responded that she would tell him in the morning which way her brother was going, and the giant left before her brother came home.

In the evening when her brother arrived, his little sister was very sweet to him. When they sat down to eat, the girl said, "Dear brother, which way are you going tomorrow?"

"Aha!" exclaimed the boy. "You're going to betray me!"

"Why do you think that?" said the girl. "No! When have I ever wanted to betray my brother?"

"OK," said the boy. "Tomorrow I'm going in the direction of the white mesa."

That night the boy didn't sleep all night, thinking of how his sister might betray him. But the next day he went out with his little animals and his rifle as usual.

Soon after the boy had left, the giant arrived, and the girl told him which way the boy had gone. The giant went off right away toward the white mesa, and when the poor boy saw the giant coming he knew instantly that his sister had betrayed him. The giant started to fight with the boy. The boy fired shots at him, but the giant carried a balm that he put on the bullet wounds, making them go away.

After a while the boy grew tired of fighting with the giant, and he called to his little animals, saying, "Now is the time to defend your dear master. Devour that giant!"

Don José the bear quickly took away the bottle of balm from the giant and threw it against a rock, and in a minute the three animals had killed the giant. After the giant fell dead, the boy told the animals, "Now, let's go have a talk with that sister of mine!"

When they arrived at the house, the boy saw the giant's tracks in the yard. He entered the house and said to his sister, "Good-bye, little sister, I'm going. I see that you don't want to be with me. You are a traitor. I killed the giant, and now you will be alone—and may God help you." The girl cried and

begged him not to go, but he called to his animals, and they all left.

They walked for a long time until they came to the house of an old woman on the edge of a city. The boy knocked at the door and asked the woman for lodging.

"You are welcome to stay with me as long as you like," she said. "I'm lonely and would like the company of you and your animal friends."

"Thank you, Grandmother," the boy said. "Can we perhaps repay you by providing you with meat to eat?"

"Yes, I would like that," the old woman replied.

Then the boy ordered his little animals to the mountains to get a deer. They returned right away with a fat, young buck.

The old woman built a fire and cooked the meat, and they all sat down to eat. As they were eating, the boy asked, "What's new in the town, Grandmother?"

The old woman replied, "There's nothing new except that there is a snake that demands that we give it a young maiden to eat every day. There are no more young girls except the princess, and tomorrow the serpent is going to eat her. The king has sworn that whoever kills this snake will marry his daughter, but so far no one has dared."

Right away the boy looked at his animal friends and said, "I'm going to marry the princess."

The next day soon after rising he went to see the princess. As he arrived he saw her seated on the balcony waiting for the serpent to come and eat her. "What are you doing there so sad?" the boy asked her.

"Ah," said the princess, "I am waiting for a serpent who is coming to eat me."

Then the boy told her, "If you will marry me, I will dare to kill the serpent."

The girl said, "Go on then! I am afraid that if you stay here any longer it will eat you along with me!"

"Don't be afraid," the boy told her. "If you promise to marry me, I will kill it."

So the princess promised to marry him, and when the serpent came for her, the boy called to his little animal friends and said, "Don León, Don Tigre, and Don José, devour that serpent!"

As quick as the wind the animals killed the snake. This serpent had seven heads, and the boy cut off the seven tongues and told Don José to swallow them. Then they went and told the princess that they had slain the serpent.

She came from the castle to see for herself, and when she saw the dead snake she gave the boy a scarf and a ring.

"These are signs of my promise to marry you," she told the boy, who accepted and said he would return the next day. Then he went back to the old woman's house, and the princess went to the king's castle.

A little while later a Moor passed by the dead snake, climbed down from his burro, and cut off its seven heads. Then he went on his way. When he came near to the princess, he said to her, "I have killed the serpent, and tomorrow you must marry me."

The princess just laughed without saying anything to the Moor. She didn't know that he had cut off the snake's heads and was on his way to tell the king that he had killed the snake.

When the king saw the seven heads of the serpent, he said to the Moor, "You will marry the princess after we celebrate for three days." Then he announced the news to everyone and told his servants to prepare the feast.

The next day the feast began, and the boy found out about it. He asked the old woman, "Do you want to have a feast?"

"With pleasure, my grandson," answered the old woman. Then the boy called to the tiger and ordered him to go to the king's castle and give the princess the scarf that she had given the boy the day before. The boy placed a little card inside the scarf, and he gave it to the tiger, reminding him not to offend anyone at the castle. The tiger went on his way, and when he came to the ballroom everyone was astonished to see that this animal went directly to where the princess was seated.

The princess took the scarf from him and read the card. Then she filled the scarf with food from the feast and gave it to the tiger. The king cried out, "I will give five pesos to whoever can tell me where that animal goes!"

All the boys at the feast went after the tiger, but as he was arriving at the old woman's house he turned around and pretended that he was going to attack them. So the boys took off running right back to the feast.

The next day, the second day of the feast, the boy told the lion to do the same thing that the tiger had done. So the lion gave the princess the scarf, she filled it with food, and presented it to the lion to bring back to the boy. When the lion was going to leave, the king once again offered five pesos to anyone who could tell him where the animal went. All the boys at the feast chased the lion, but he did the same thing as the tiger—he turned around and growled ferociously, pretending that he was going to attack them. The terrified boys took off running right back to the feast and told the king that they couldn't follow the lion.

The next day was the final day of the feast, and the boy called to Don José the bear and told him, "Now you go to the feast, and don't get drunk, do you hear me?"

Don José shook his head that he understood. When he arrived at the feast, all the people were frightened and scurried to one side of the room. Don José went directly to where the princess was seated and presented her with the scarf. Then the princess took Don José to the banquet accompanied by the king, the queen, and the Moor, whom she was to marry.

When they were seated at the banquet table, the king began to pour wine for Don José and kept pouring until Don José was drunk. Then he gave the bear a barrel of wine and the scarf filled with food.

Because Don José was drunk, he walked away stumbling and falling, and the boys were able to follow him to the old woman's house. Then they returned to the castle to tell the king where Don José had gone. The king told them that the next day they were going to have one more day of feasting and that the boys should go and invite the master of the animals. Right away the servants went and invited the boy and the old woman.

The next day when the boy arrived at the king's castle he told the king that he wanted to talk with him alone. After the boy and the king went into a room and began to converse, the boy told the king, "Your Majesty, have you seen bells without clappers?"

"No," said the king. "Why do you ask me that?"

"Oh," said the young man, "just because I want to know if you have seen bells without clappers." Then he said, "And have you seen heads without tongues?"

"No," answered the king.

Then the boy said to the king, "Bring me the serpent's heads to see if they have tongues."

Also the boy called to Don José and told him to bring the tongues from the serpent's heads. When the king saw the heads without tongues and the tongues that the bear brought, he called in the Moor and told him that he wasn't going to marry his daughter because he hadn't killed the serpent. Instead, he ordered the Moor to go to work, and the Moor left, crying, "The serpent has no tongues, the serpent has no tongues!" Then the king told the master of the animals that, since he was the one who had killed the serpent, he would marry the princess. And the king announced three more days of feasting.

Three days of feasting followed. On the day when the boy and the princess were going to get married, the young man's sister suddenly appeared in the castle, having studied magic books during the time she was alone. She had grown bitter and jealous living all alone and had come to kill her brother. When she first arrived, she acted nice and told the king that she wanted to see her brother alone in a room. After the boy entered the room with her, the girl began to talk sweetly to him. Then suddenly she took out the canine teeth of the giant, which she had carried with her, and stuck them into the boy.

As soon as the teeth entered his body, the boy died, and his sister disappeared and went away to the mountains. After a while the king saw that the boy had not left the room, and he went in to find him dead. He couldn't tell what had killed the boy, and everyone, especially the princess, cried a lot when they found out that the boy was dead.

The next day they had a grand funeral and buried the boy. The king was afraid that the boy's animal friends would act wild, now that the boy wasn't around to control them, so he ordered his servants to lock them in a room in the castle. The poor animals were left behind and didn't see their dead master.

In three days the king unlocked the door to their room and set the animals free. Right away they ran to look for their master. They sniffed the ground and followed the footprints of all the people who had gone to the cemetery. When they came to the boy's grave, they dug until they unearthed their dear master and cried bitterly.

Then Don José began to caress the boy's body and noticed something strange. He felt closely until he discovered the giant's teeth. He pulled them out, and the boy rose up, alive!

Then the boy went with the animals back to the king's castle. Everyone was astonished when they saw him, but he told them not to fear, that his sister had bewitched him with the giant's teeth. He related the whole story of his sister and how she had betrayed him to the giant. The king was glad that the boy was back, but no one was as happy as the princess. From that day on, the prince never saw his sister again. He and the princess and his little animal friends lived happily together for many years. Perhaps they're still living happily.

Y colorín colorado	*Y él que no se levanta*
And red and redder	And he who doesn't get up
Este cuento se ha acabado	*Se quedará pegado!*
This cuento has ended	Will remain stuck in place! ✛

"I've never heard that cuento before," says Grandma, and I'm shocked because I thought she knew all the cuentos ever told. Tía Juanita says she doesn't remember where it came from but that Reyes probably told it to her when he was an old man.

"No," says Grandma with certainty. "He never told us that story, but it's a good one." Grandma takes a last look around the house, peering for a moment into the bedroom where she was born and where her mother died, shaking her head but uttering not a word before we say our good-byes to Tía Juanita and walk back across the road to home.

And ever after that day, Grandma can easily tell me, from memory, the story of El Oso Don José just as tía Juanita had read it.

Juan Burumbete

Grandma, 102 years old, lies in bed with her eyes closed and a peaceful expression on her face. I walk into her room, freshly painted in bright turquoise just the week before in anticipation of her birthday celebration. This is her "new" room, the one on the south side of the house where she moved last year to be closer to the warming sun of winter. Before she always had stayed in the cold north-facing room to avoid the summer sun.

Grandma's husband died in this room fifty-one years ago on a cold October day. I remember well the story of his death when he was only forty-eight, not that Grandma dwells on it but because she used it to frighten me into wearing a jacket when I went outside. The scenario has been drilled into me until I can see it unfold as if I'd been there. On that fateful day, Grandpa went out in his shirtsleeves to visit David and other primos at the weaving shop across the street, where he sold the blankets that he wove. He came home feeling chilled and with a strange pallor to his skin, slumped onto the bed, and announced, "Today, I'm going to kick the bucket," using the American phrase that he had learned from his Anglo buddies in Durango, Colorado. Before long he let out a gasp, clutched his chest, and was gone.

Grandma and I never stayed in this room in the summers of my youth, and it seems strange to see her here. Knowing the room's history, it makes me nervous and apprehensive. Has she moved here in anticipation of leaving this world? Grandma doesn't like the new room much, either, and feels out of place, but she knows it's better for her. She can't walk now and is always cold, even on warm summer days. She passes most of her time in bed, and the old stories are getting farther and farther away from her.

I walk in, and she doesn't open her eyes, as if she doesn't want to expend the energy of looking up and seeing who I am, which would be difficult in any case. Her eyes are failing, and she can only perceive shapes and lights and darks. Despite these limitations, she usually knows me because I'm the tallest person in her daily life. In fact, she tells me that I look a lot like her father, Reyes. One time at the kitchen table she started suddenly and looked at me aghast. When I asked her what was wrong, she said, "I thought I was sitting here with my father. You look and sit just like him."

Finally, Grandma calls out, "Quién viene? Who's coming?"

"Soy Juan Burumbete," I say, and she breaks into a wide grin and, without missing a beat, repeats the next line of the story: "Con un moquete mata a siete, y con un rempujón, un montón!"

Then we break out laughing, remembering the story of Juan Burumbete and traveling back together to those summer evenings when she told it to me. Whenever I didn't want to take a bath, which was often, Grandma would bring up this unclean character, using his name as a warning to all who would be lazy and unclean. She'd say, "Bueno, so you don't want to take a bath? Do you remember Juan Burumbete? I've told you that story, que no?"

And I'd always answer, hoping to put off the inevitable dunk in water, sometimes with lye soap that Grandma had made, "No, Grandma, I don't remember Juan Burumbete. Who was he?"

Now, Grandma closes her eyes and says; "Tell me the story." It's my turn to tell the story to Grandma as she lies like a child, helpless in bed. I manage to tell it in the Spanish I've slowly learned from her over my lifetime, in large part by listening to these cuentos.

WELL, ONCE THERE LIVED THIS MAN named Juan Burumbete. This Juan was so lazy that he didn't even have the motivation to bathe himself, so he was always filthy. He just sat in his filth and didn't even notice it.

One summer day Juan was sitting in the sun covered with flies, as usual, because flies love filth, you know. The flies were bothering Juan, and he was slapping them every now and then, not too fast because he didn't want to tire himself. After a while he began to get angry with the flies and tried harder to get rid of them. He sat there and counted every fly he swatted. He slapped his face and killed seven flies at once. Then he slapped his arm and killed eleven more.

"Oh!" said Juan. "I'm very brave. With one blow I kill seven, and with another blow I kill eleven!"

Juan sat there saying this to himself over and over again. So pleased was he with his accomplishment that he went to the blacksmith shop and asked the blacksmith to make him a sign to put on his hat. The sign said:

This is Juan Burumbete
With one blow he kills seven
And with another blow he kills eleven.

Then Juan sat out at his usual place by the Camino Real to watch people go by, feeling very good about himself. When people saw him sitting there and read the sign on his hat, their eyes opened wide, and they ran away. They thought the sign meant that Juan had killed many people, not flies, and they were afraid that he would kill them, too.

Some of the people who saw Juan reported to the king that there was a brave and dangerous man in the kingdom—one who was an expert at ways of killing. When the king heard about Juan, his eyes widened, and he said, "God has heard my prayers! The Moors killed my son, Macario, and if this man is as brave as my son he can avenge my son's death."

So the king sent for Juan, who was still sitting in the sun by the Camino Real swatting flies. He was so lazy that he hadn't gone anywhere! Juan was surprised to hear that the king wanted to see him, but he followed the king's servant down the road to the castle.

When they arrived, the king asked, "Are you really as brave as your sign claims you are?"

"Yes, Your Majesty, with one blow I can kill seven, and with another blow I can kill eleven," Juan answered.

"All right then," the king said. "I want you to get ready to fight against the Moors as soon as you can. And if you are victorious I'll give you my daughter, the princess, in marriage."

Juan was afraid to tell the king that it was only flies he had killed, so he just said, "Yes, Your Majesty," and then he left for his home.

The next day Juan returned to the king's castle. The king gave him a fine horse that had belonged to his son, Macario. This horse was big and proud and pranced around with his head up in the air. "You see," said the king, "Macario's horse is ready to avenge his master's death! He will carry you swiftly into battle!"

Juan looked at the giant beast and shook with fear. He had never mounted a horse of any kind, much less a spirited war-horse. How was he going to keep the soldiers from seeing his ignorance and fear? He thought for a minute and then told the soldiers, "All right, my friends, tie me on my horse!"

The soldiers were shocked and said to one another, "*Qué tiene ese hombre?* How is this man going to fight if he's tied up?" But they did what Juan told them, and Juan clung to the saddle horn with both hands. The people shook their heads in disbelief, but they saw the sign on Juan's hat and thought he must have some trick up his sleeve. Then Juan and the soldiers rode off across the plain in a cloud of dust.

They rode for a long time, and Juan's rear end began to get sore. He wanted to get off the horse, but he knew he couldn't turn back, and anyway he was tied on the saddle. Approaching the battlefield, he was tired and sore all over. He began to worry and thought, "What am I going to do so that my companions won't know that I am a coward and don't know how to ride a horse, much less fight on one?" By the time they reached the battlefield, Juan had a solution. He stopped the other soldiers and told them, "I don't want you to go with me. I'll go on alone. Wait here for me."

The soldiers were astonished, but they let Juan go ahead into battle. He rode until he came to a deep canyon near the place where the Moors were waiting. When Macario's horse heard the battle cry go up from the Moors, he reared on his hind legs because he was an experienced war-horse and had fought with the Moors many times. Juan became terrified and began to cry out in a loud voice, saying, "Oh God, this *caballo* is going to take my life!"

The Moors heard Juan's cry but thought he had said, "Macario has been revived!" They recognized Macario's horse and were so frightened to think that Macario had risen from the dead that they took off in retreat. In their haste they didn't watch where they were going, and they all fell into the canyon and were killed.

When Juan saw what had happened, he went back to his waiting comrades and said, "Well, I've killed all the Moors already."

The soldiers couldn't believe him. "How could you have done that so quickly?" they asked, and they rode to the battlefield to see for themselves. Then after they looked in the canyon and saw all the Moors and their horses dead at the bottom they quickly sent a messenger to notify the king of Juan's victory.

The king was happy to hear that the Moors had been defeated. "At last Macario's death has been avenged. May he rest in peace," said the king. Then

he called for his daughter and told her, "I promised Juan Burumbete that he could marry you if he won the battle, and he has done just that."

The princess burst out crying. "I'm not going to marry that filthy man!" she sobbed.

"Don't worry, my daughter," said the king. "That illness has a remedy."

Then the king made Juan take a good, hot bath in lye soap and gave him a fine suit of clothes to wear. After Juan emerged, he no longer looked like the filthy Juan Burumbete, and, amazingly, he was no longer lazy. When the princess saw how handsome he looked, she stopped grumbling. She and Juan married and lived happily for the rest of their lives.

Grandma seems to be sleeping and doesn't say a word. I'm about to leave when she speaks, "You know that story so well, 'jito. I guess I taught you pretty good, eh? The only thing is that this Juan, he wasn't just handsome after that bath, he was smarter, too. He had more self-respect, see, because he took care of himself and looked good, and that made people respect him, too. That's why I'm always telling you not to go around so greñudo."

Benigna Recuerda

Pascual Ranchero

Cuanto hay había un Padre que vivía cerca del rey. Su casa tenía un portal mure largo y ahí andaba él pensando y rezando el rosario todas las tardes. Un día estaba el rey mirándolo de su balcón y al estar cuidando el rey al padre él pensó en si mismo:

—Ese Padre quizás sea muy vivo. Yo me tengo que desengañar si es tan vivo como parece.

Pues, el rey llamó a uno de sus sirvientes y le dijo:

—Ve a casa del Padre y dile que el rey lo quiere ver.

Fue el sirviente y le dio el mensaje al Padre. El Padre estaba muy contento porque lo llamó el rey y pronto fue a ver qué quería. Se sentía muy importante y muy orgulloso.

Cuando llegó el Padre al castillo y se presentó al rey, el rey le dijo:

—Yo lo he estado cuidando hace muncho tiempo y parece que usted es un hombre muy vivo. Para saber de cierto si es tan vivo como parece, le voy a hacer tres preguntas, y si no las responde dentro de una semana, pena de la vida.

—O, no será difícil saber —pensó el Padre—. Tengo munchos libros y estoy seguro de que puedo contestar cualquier pregunta del rey.

Dijo el rey:

—La primera pregunta es, ¿cuánto tiempo me tardaré para llegar al cabito del mundo? La segunda es, ¿cuánto es mi valor? Y la tercera, ¿cuál es mi pensamiento?

El Padre se fue a su casa y pronto se puso a estudiar los libros que tenía a ver si hallaba las respuestas para las preguntas. Cuando vido que no hallaba las respuestas en ninguno de sus libros, sabía que de seguro lo mataría el rey. Pensó salir de allí para que no lo matara el rey. Bajó el escalerado y le dijo a su cocinera que iba a ir a pasear por unos días. Asina no se daría cuenta nadien que se había ido huyendo. En la madrugada ensilló a su caballo y se fue caminando todo el día. Muy noche se encontró con un pastor cuidando a sus borregas.

—Padre, ¿Qué anda haciendo por estos rumbos? —preguntó el pastor.

Entonces el Padre se dio cuenta que no era otro más que Pascual Ranchero, el pastor que cuidaba a sus borregas. El padre no le contestó. Sólo meneaba la cabeza muy triste. Pronto Pascual malició que algo tenía el Padre y le dijo:

—Bájese del caballo, Padre, y siéntese junto a la lumbre. Pase la noche aquí conmigo y descanse.

Pascual mató un borreguito y asó la carne en las brasas y llamó al Padre a comer. El Padre después de sólo un bocado no comía más. Pascual lo vía muy pensativo y le preguntó:

—¿Por qué está tan pensativo, Padre?

—Sabes, Pascual —le dijo el Padre—, que no me siento muy bien. Tengo dolor de estómago.

—Por eso no se acongoje Padre, ahora mismo voy por hierbas de remedio para hervirle —le respondió

Pascual Ranchero.

Fue y le trujo estafiate y le hizo un té, pero no le hizo el remedio nada bien al Padre. Otro día, muy de mañana, se levantó Pascual Ranchero muy contento. Él cantaba y chiflaba mientras alistaba el almuerzo. Pensó el Padre:

—¡Bendito sea Dios! Este joven tan pobre y solo y tan contento que anda, y yo que tengo todo tan triste que me siento.

En esto lo llamó Pascual a comer y le dijo:

—Mire, Padre, qué bueno está el café y la carne asada.

Pero el Padre no comía, solo clavaba la vista al suelo y pintaba rayas en la tierra.

—Padre, usted no está enfermo —dijo Pascual—. Usted tiene una pena y no quiere confiar en mí. Dígame, Padre, ¿qué le pasa? Pueda que yo le pueda ayudar.

—Yo que sé muncho más que tú y no puedo ayudarme solo, y ¿qué vas a poder tú que no eres más que un pastor? —respondió el Padre.

—Nada pierde con decirme.

—Bueno —dijo el Padre—, voy a decirte todo, asina descansa mi pecho, mas que no me puedas ayudar de otro modo. —Pues, le platicó todo y terminó diciendo:

—Estas preguntas son tan difíciles que no hay manera de contestarlas.

Pues —dijo Pascual—, ¿cuáles son las preguntas?

—¿Para qué quieres saber si ni yo mismo las encontré en ninguno de mis libros? Pero sí te las diré —le dijo el Padre—. La primera es, ¿cuánto tiempo me dilataré para llegar al cabito del mundo? La segunda, ¿cuánto es mi valor? Y la tercera, ¿cuál es mi pensamiento?

Soltó la risa Pascual y dijo:

—¿En tan poca agua se hoga?

—¡No me digas que tú sabes las respuestas! — exclamó el Padre.

—Seguro que sí —respondió Pascual.

—Pues dímelas a mí.

—No puedo decírselas ahora porque las paredes tienen oídos y los sabinos sentidos —dijo Pascual muy calladito—. Yo le diré lo que hacemos. Mañana muy de mañanita nos vamos para su casa y luego le digo.

El Padre no quería volver a casa porque estaba cierto que Pascual no sabía las respuestas y que el rey lo horcaría. Pero al fin convino el Padre de salir otro día. Caminaron todo el día bajando la montaña y llegaron a la casa del Padre muy noche. Pascual se durmió tan pronto como se acostó. El Padre no durmió nada.

Otro día se levantó el Padre muy de mañana. Pascual todavía estaba roncando. El Padre fue a despertarlo.

—Pascual, ¿cómo puedes dormir? ¿No estás apenado?

—Bueno, pues, Padre, pero ¿por qué tanta prisa? El rey puede esperar un tiempo. —Pascual se levantó, estirándose y le dijo:

—Padre, ahora tiene que cambiar vestido conmigo.

—¡Ay Dios! ¿Qué estará pensando hacer este hombre? —pensó el Padre. Pero, estaba a la misericordia de Pascual y quiso que no quiso cambió vestidos con él.

Pronto se caminaron al castillo del rey. La gente se había dado cuenta de que éste era el día que tenía que aparecerse el Padre delante del rey. Ya estaban allí esperando a ver si el rey mandaría que el Padre fuera horcado.

Cuando entraron el Padre y Pascual Ranchero al castillo le dijo el rey a Pascual, pensando que era el Padre:

—Pase p'acá delante.

Y al Padre, pensando que era Pascual:

—Y tú, Pascual, siéntate detrás de la puerta.

Entonces le preguntó a Pascual:

—Padre, ¿Ya está listo para contestar las preguntas?

—¿Sabe qué? —respondió Pascual—. ¡Ya se me olvidaron! Dígamelas otra vez.

—¡Se le olvidaron! —exclamó el rey. No creía lo que estaba oyendo.

—No pensé muncho en ellas —dijo Pascual.

—Bueno, pues —dijo el rey—. Ésta es la primera, ¿cuánto tiempo me tardaré para llegar al cabito del mundo?

Pascual respondió inmediatamente:

—Si camina a par del sol llegará en un día.

Toda la gente se miraron muy sorprendidos porque le respondió bien y el rey tuvo que aceptarlo.

—Respondió bien, muy bien —dijo el rey—. La segunda es, ¿cuánto es mi valor?

Todos se quedaron muy callados porque sabían que el rey pensaba que tenía muncho valor. Si el Padre dijiera muy poco, el rey se pondría nojado, pero si el Padre dijiera muncho, daría la impresión de que el rey era avariento.

—Pues su valor no es nada porque solamente a Jesucristo lo vendió Judas Escariote por treinta monedas de plata —respondió Pascual.

Todos sabían que eso era la verdad. ¿Cómo podría un buen cristiano como el rey decir que tenía valor en comparación a Jesucristo?

—Buena respuesta —dijo el rey—. Pero todavía le falta responder una pregunta más, y si no la responde, pena de la vida. La tercera es, ¿cuál es mi pensamiento?

Pascual sonrió y le dijo:

—Pues su pensamiento es que yo soy el Padre pero soy Pascual Ranchero y ¡ése que está detrás de la puerta es el Padre!

El rey no pudo más que soltar la risa y la gente junto con él. Luego todos empezaron a traquear las manos. Salió el Padre de allí muy contento porque había salido con bien. Más tarde le dijo a Pascual:

—Pascual, tú me salvates la vida y no quiero que te vayas a cuidar a mis borregas jamás. Que otro muchacho lo haga.

—Padre, le agradezco muncho, pero yo estoy más feliz viviendo solo en el monte cuidando a mis borreguitos —respondió Pascual Ranchero.

Se subió en su mulita y se fue muy contento para el monte chiflando y cantando. ✛

La Tierra de Mogolló

Cuanto hay había un hombre muy trabajador y todos los días iba al monte con su burro por su carga de leña que luego vendía en la ciudad. Tenía tres hijas pero no tenía hijos, entonces iba a cortar leña solo. Una hija, su favorita, siempre quería ir con él porque le encantaba ir al monte a ver los pinabetes. Pero como era muncho trabajo ir al monte y no era un lugar para jugar, le decía:

—No, mi jita, está lejos y tengo muncho trabajo que hacer. No es un lugar para una joven. Ya estoy saliendo, pero mañana pueda que sí vayas conmigo.

Ese día estaba cortando un pino cuando le salió un lagarto de abajo del troncón. El hombre se espantó muncho cuando vido al lagarto que le habló diciendo:

—¡Yo te voy a comer!

—¡Por favor de Dios! —le suplicó el hombre—, ¡no me comas!

—Pues, ¿qué me das si no te como?

—No tengo nada que darte, pues soy hombre pobre.

—¿Tienes familia? —le preguntó el lagarto.

—Tengo tres hijas.

—Pues no te como si mañana me traes a tu hija favorita —dijo el lagarto.

El hombre se fue muy triste para su casa pues no quería perder a ninguna de sus hijas, mayormente a su favorita que le había dicho:

—Recuerda, papá que mañana voy contigo al monte.

Otro día se levantó el hombre muy de mañana para tratar de salir sin ella, pero ya había preparado la hija comida para llevar al monte. Pues se fueron para el bosque, al mismo lugar en donde apareció el lagarto el día antes. Al comienzo el hombre no vido al lagarto por ninguna parte y pensó:

—Tal vez se olvidó de mi promesa ayer.

Pero cuando se puso a cortar un pino y el lagarto se le aprontó otra vez y le preguntó:

—¿Vino tu hija contigo?

—Sí —respondió el hombre. —Llamó a su hija que estaba poco retirada de allí pepenando flores, y le dijo:

—Hijita mía, tengo que entregarte a este lagarto o si no, me come.

Cuando vido la hija al lagarto le dio muncho miedo de verlo tan feo, pero como era una hija obediente, le dijo a su papá:

—Yo haré lo que usted me mande en tal de que no se lo coma este lagarto. —Ella sabía que tenía que hacer todo lo que su padre le mandaba, a pesar de que no quería ir con el lagarto.

Se dijieron adiós el padre y la hija y se fue el padre muy triste para su casa. Ya cuando no vía más al hombre, el lagarto le dijo a la joven:

—Súbete en mi lomo y préndete bien, cierra los

ojos y no los abras hasta que yo te diga.

La muchacha hizo lo que el lagarto le mandó. Agarró bien ese cuero feo y rasposo y se prendió bien y los dos desaparecieron debajo del troncón. De repente la joven se sentía como si estuviera volando en el cielo en medio de un viento fuerte y quería abrir los ojos. Finalmente, no aguantaba más y abrió los ojos un poquito y vido las estrellas arriba y la tierra abajo muy lejos. Cerró bien los ojos otra vez. Después de un tiempo, el lagarto le dijo que podía abrir los ojos y cuando los abrió se halló en un palacio muy hermoso con jardines verdes y flores por todas partes. Era el lugar más bonito que había visto .

Llegaron muy tarde y ya llegaba la noche. El lagarto le dijo:

—¿Tienes hambre? Hay comida para ti. —Pero la joven no tenía nada de hambre. Al ver que no comía, el lagarto la llevó a un cuarto muy grande con una cama grande en medio y un fogón en el rincón.

Ella miró todo y pensó:

—¿Cómo es que un animal tan feo puede llegar a ser tan rico?

Deseaba vivir en un lugar asina. Pues eran muy pobres ella y su padre y vivían en una casa pequeñita sin ventanas ni muebles.

El lagarto le hablaba bonito a la joven y poco a poco ya no le tenía miedo, aunque era un animal tan feo. De repente se sentía la joven muy cansada y se acostó a dormir en la cama. El lagarto estaba cerca del fogón, mirando las llamas y esperando que ella se durmiera. Cuando ella se cerró los ojos, él se quitó el cuero de lagarto y ¡se volvió un joven muy bien parecido! La muchacha estaba haciéndose la dormida y vido todo lo que pasó. Llevó muncho gusto en ver que el lagarto feo era en realidad un joven muy hermoso.

—Voy a ver qué hago con esa piel fea —pensó ella al dormirse.

La siguiente noche pasó la misma cosa. La muchacha pretendía que estaba dormida otra vez,

pero esta vez cuando el joven se acostó, se levantó la muchacha y agarró el cuero y lo echó en la lumbre. Estaba traqueando tanto el cuero en la lumbre que se despertó el joven. Se saltó de la cama y dijo:

—¡O, no! ¡Mira lo que has hecho! Todo está perdido.

—Pero, ¿qué tienes? —le preguntó la joven.

—Yo en verdad soy un príncipe y éste es el castillo de mi padre, pero hace muncho tiempo que una bruja me embrujó —explicó el príncipe—. Ella me permitió quedarme aquí sólo si yo llevara ese cuero durante el día para que ninguna mujer me viera.

—¿Y qué? —dijo la joven—. Ahora podemos vivir juntos y yo estaré feliz porque eres un joven muy guapo.

—No, no. Escucha. Ahora que me quemates el cuero del lagarto seré prisionero de ella en la Tierra de Mogolló. Tengo que irme en cuanto el sol salga para quedarme con ella en ese lugar desolado.

El príncipe se sentía triste porque tenía que salir del palacio y dejar a la joven. Antes de la madrugada, la despertó y le dijo:

—Siento muncho dejarte sola, pero te dejo algo para acordarte de mí. Tal vez te ayude.

Él abrió una caja grande y sacó una bota. El príncipe luego le explicó:

—Esta botita te llevará adonde quieras. No tienes más que decirle, "Cuela botita," y decirle adónde quieres ir y caminarán invisibles.

Tan pronto como le dio la botita, se desaparecieron el príncipe y el castillo y se fue dejando a la joven sola en un desierto sin nadien. Estaba muy triste y no sabía qué hacer. No tenía su padre con ella ni sabía adónde ir.

—Yo voy a buscar la Tierra de Mogolló a encontrar al príncipe —decidió ella—. Pero no sé cómo llegar a ese lugar. Pueda que la luna sepa, pues está alta en el cielo y ve todo. —La joven se metió en la bota y dijo:

—Cuela botita, cuela botita, ¡llévame a la tierra de la luna!

Pronto se fue volando la botita muy alto en el cielo hasta que llegaron al lugar de la luna, pero la luna no estaba allá. Pero sí estaban las lunitas bailando en el cielo oscuro y lleno de estrellas. La joven les preguntó:

—Ando buscando la tierra de Mogolló. ¿No saben dónde está?

—No —le contestaron—, pero pueda que nuestra mamá, la luna, sepa. Está viajando en el otro lado de la tierra, pero vuelve pronto.

A poco rato llegó la luna muy brillante.

—¡Hola, hola! A carne humana me huele aquí, y si no me la das, comerte a ti —dijo la luna. La joven se saltó para atrás, casi muerta de miedo de la luna.

—¡No! —le contestaron las lunitas—, no se la comas, que sólo es una pobre joven que anda preguntando por la tierra de Mogolló. ¿No sabe usted dónde está?

La luna arrugó la frente y se puso a pensar antes de decir:

—No, nunca ha visto ese lugar, pero pueda que el sol sepa. Él anda de día y ve más que yo.

Entonces la joven dijo:

—Cuela, botita, ¡llévame al lugar del sol!

Pronto llegó en donde el sol vivía, pero sólo estaban los solecitos, casi como estrellitas, por todas partes. Ella les preguntó si no sabían dónde estaba la Tierra de Mogolló.

—No sabemos —dijieron ellos—, pero nuestro papá, el sol, si ha de saber pues viaja alrededor del mundo. Está en el otro lado del mundo ahora, pero vuelve pronto.

Al rato llegó el sol quemando como el fuego.

—¡Hola, hola!. A carne humana me huele aquí, y si no me la das, comerte a ti.

La joven tenía miedo como antes y tenía tanto calor que pensaba que se iba a quemar.

—No se la comas —le dijieron los solecitos—. Sólo es una pobre joven que anda en busca de la Tierra de Mogolló. ¿No sabe usted dónde está? Usted viaja por todo el mundo de día, ¿no sabe dónde está?

Después de pensar un poco él dijo:

—No, nunca he visto ese lugar, pero pueda que los aires sepan. Ellos andan en todos los rincones del mundo y ven más que yo.

Pronto se fue la joven a buscar a los aires. Le dijo a su botita:

—¡Cuela botita, cuela botita! —y se fue la botita volando hasta que llegó en donde vivían los airecitos. Ella vido que los airecitos se movían alrededor de ella y les preguntó:

—Ando buscando la Tierra de Mogolló. ¿No saben ustedes dónde está?

Los airecitos se secreteaban uno al otro y luego le dijieron:

—No, nunca hemos oído de tal tierra y nosotros andamos por todo el mundo. Mañana saldremos todos a buscar. Espéranos aquí y te daremos cuenta más tarde si la encontramos.

Otro día salieron todos. Ella se quedó sola esperándolos. Al anochecer, llegaron los airecitos de vuelta, menos uno. Se vían muy cansados.

—Todos tomamos diferentes partes del mundo y buscamos en cada rincón —le dijieron—, y no pudimos hallar la Tierra de Mogolló.

La joven estaba muy desafusiada y pensaba que nunca iba a encontrar la Tierra de Mogolló. Pensó:

—Si la luna y el sol y todos los aires no sabían dónde estaba, ¿a quién más le puedo preguntar? ¿Cómo puedo hallarlo?

En ese momento llegó el último airecito ya cuando estaba muy noche. Estaba muy cansado y apenas se movía. Le dijo en voz baja a la joven:

—Me anduve buscando la Tierra de Mogolló todo el día y la mitad le la noche, y al fin la hallé en el último rincón del mundo. Mañana te llevo p'allá si es que de veras quieres ir a un lugar tan desolado y triste. —Nadien quería ir a la Tierra de Mogolló pues estaba tan lejos y era un lugar muy desolado.

—Seguro que sí quiero ir —dijo la joven. Le daba ansias pensar que el príncipe estuviera en un lugar tan feo. Ya para el otro día, cuando los airecitos apenas empezaban a moverse, ella se metió en la botita y dijo:

—Botita, botita, ¡sigue al airecito a la Tierra de Mogolló!

Se fue volando la botita siguiendo al airecito. Viajaron todo el día hasta llegar al último rincón del mundo, y ya cuando fueron aun más, llegaron a la Tierra de Mogolló.

Hacía muncho frío y estaba muy feo y oscuro, pues el sol y la luna nunca habían brillado en la Tierra de Mogolló. Había nomás que una casa sola en esa tierra desolada y allí andaba la bruja fuera de la casa pepenando leña. Era muy mala la bruja y cuando oyó el airecito, volteó la cabeza y dijo:

—¿Airecitos en la Tierra de Mogolló? ¡Nunca los había visto yo! —Pues ni un airecito había pasado por ese lugar.

—Aquí te dejo —le dijo el airecito a la joven—. Que te vaya bien en este destierro.

Y asina se fue el airecito, dejando a la joven en la oscuridad, fuera de la casa de la bruja. No había casi ninguna cosa viva por allí, sólo arena y piedras y algunos coyotes.

Pronto entró la vieja bruja a la casa y la siguió la joven. Estaba invisible, pues estaba en su botita, entonces la bruja no se dio cuenta de que estaba otra persona con ella en la cocina. La bruja echó leña en el fogón y se puso a hacer buñuelos, riéndose solita mientras amasaba la masa. La joven la miraba y como traiba muncha hambre, fue a la mesa y se puso a comer buñuelos. La bruja estaba hacer y hacer buñuelos y la joven estaba comer y comer, hasta que al fin exclamó la bruja:

—Pues ¿qué es esto? ¡Tanta buñuelada para mi perrada y que no rinda yo!

Tan pronto como los hacía, la joven los comía. Por fin, la joven estaba llena y la bruja tenía un plato lleno de buñuelos. Agarró unas llaves y llevó el plato de buñuelos con ella. La joven se fue detrás de ella en su botita. Entraron en un zaguán en donde había munchos cuartos atrancados. En cada cuarto estaba un príncipe embrujado por la vieja bruja. Estaban muy tristes en sus cuartos, pero como estaban embrujados, no podían hacer nada.

La bruja se fue cuarto por cuarto, dándoles los buñuelos a los hombres como si fueran perros. Se reía cuando agarraban los pedacitos de comida porque tenían tanta hambre. Cuando llegó al cuarto del príncipe, estaba él adentro. La joven se quedó en el cuarto con él, y tan pronto como la bruja se fue, ella salió de la botita y apareció al príncipe. Cuando la vido el príncipe se quiso morir de gusto, y le preguntó:

—¿Cómo llegates aquí?

—Seguí a la bruja —le contestó ella.

—Pero ¿Cómo llegates a la Tierra de Mogolló? — dijo el príncipe.

Ella le contó todo lo que había pasado. Entonces, de repente el príncipe se puso triste.

—¿Por qué venites aquí? —le preguntó muy quedito para que la bruja no pudiera oír—. Ahora la bruja va a encontrarte y embrujarte también. Te va a poner en uno de estos cuartos y nunca podrás salir de esta fea Tierra de Mogolló.

—Pues dime cómo hacer para sacarte de aquí — le dijo la joven.

—Bueno, te diré —respondió el príncipe—. Solamente de un modo puedes sacarme de aquí. Pero es muy peligroso. La bruja tiene dos huevos en el trastero en la cocina. En estos huevos tiene su vida. Va a ser difícil de alcanzar ese trastero, pues ella guarda esos huevos con muncho cuidado. Pero si puedes, ¡agarra estos huevos y quiébralos! Eso será el fin de esa bruja.

Otro día cuando fue la bruja a darles de comer a sus cautivos, fue la joven a la cocina en su botita. Tuvo que salir de su botita y se subió en una silleta para alcanzar a agarrar los huevos del trastero. Tan pronto como salió de su botita ya no estaba invisible. Abrió el trastero y en este momento escuchó las llaves de la bruja y la oyó hablando mientras entraba en la cocina después de darles de comer a sus prisioneros. La joven subió apriesa, pero tenía que estirarse hasta la parte de atrás del trastero. En ese momento entró la bruja y gritó:

—¿Quién eres tú? ¿Y qué andas haciendo en ese trastero?

La bruja agarró a la joven del pescuezo con sus dedos flacos a la misma hora que la joven agarró los huevos y los tiró en el suelo. Tan pronto como se quebraron, cayó la bruja muerta y la Tierra de Mogolló se llenó de calor y luz, pues sin el poder de la bruja, el sol y la luna podían brillar otra vez. Agarró las llaves la joven y se fue a sacar al príncipe de su cuarto.

—¿Cómo matates a la bruja? —le preguntó.

—Nomás hice lo que tú me mandates hacer —dijo la joven.

Luego fueron él y ella y abrieron las demás puertas en donde estaban los otros jóvenes prisioneros. Todos salieron muy contentos porque ya no estaban bajo el poder de la bruja. Partieron para sus casas que ya no estaban tan lejos. El príncipe y la joven se metieron en la botita y dijieron:

—Cuela botita, llévanos para el palacio —y pronto llegaron al palacio con todos los jardines.

—Pensaba que nunca vería este lugar otra vez —dijo el príncipe.

El rey estaba mure contento de ver a su hijo y lo abrazó. Le dijieron al rey todo lo que había pasado y él le agradeció a la joven por haberlo rescatado de la bruja. El príncipe y la joven decidieron casarse allí mismo y vivir en el palacio, pero primero fueron por el padre de la joven para que él pudiera vivir junto con ellos.

Su padre estaba cortando leña en el monte cuando lo encontraron. Él lloró con alegría cuando vido a su hija y dijo:

—Perdóname, hija, que te di a ese lagarto feo. Me hubiera llevado a mí en vez de a ti. —Pero cuando oyó todo lo que había pasado, ya no estaba triste de haberla mandado con el lagarto.

La joven y el príncipe pronto celebraron sus bodas y vivieron felices en el castillo con los jardines bonitos. Su padre ya no tenía que ir al monte a cortar leña . . .

Y comieron perdices, y a mí me dieron con los huesos en las narices! ✛

El Viejo Tuerto

Una vez había un viejito que no vía con un ojo y le decían el viejo tuerto. Él tenía una huerta de higas y todas las tardes ya cuando se iba haciendo oscuro salía al patio de su casa y se ponía a tocar su violín y a cantar:

"En el hueco de una higuera
Tengo mis doscientos pesos
En el hueco de una higuera
Tengo mis doscientos pesos"

Una noche andaban unos muchachos robando higos y oyeron la canción que el viejito cantaba.

—¿Cómo hacemos para meterle miedo a ese viejo para poderle robar sus doscientos pesos? —dijieron ellos—. Vamos a ponernos de sábanas a ver si asina lo espantamos.

La siguiente noche vinieron todos vestidos de sábanas y se acercaron al viejito tocando su violín. Juntos se pusieron a cantar en voz alta:

"Cuanto hay cuando éranos vivos
veníamos a juntar higos
y ahora que estamos muertos
Venimos por el viejo tuerto"

Cuando los vido el viejito y oyó lo que decían le dio tanto miedo que se metió a su casa y atrancó la puerta. Otro día cuando fue a ver su dinero en el hueco de la higuera halló que ya no había nada y malició que eran unos pícaros los que le habían metido miedo la noche antes.

—¿Cómo haré yo para que estos ladrones me devuelvan mi dinero? —pensó él.

Pronto pensó cómo engañarles. Nomás se llegó la noche cuando se sentó en el patio y empezó a tocar su violín y a cantar:

"En el hueco de una higuera
Tengo mis doscientos pesos
Y doscientos que voy a poner
Son cuatrocientos"

Los mismos muchachos estaban escuchándolo. Cuando oyeron lo que él cantaba dijieron:

—El viejo tuerto no se ha dado cuenta que le robamos su dinero. ¡Vamos a ponerlo para tras y asina nos hacemos de más dinero!

Otro día muy de mañana fue el viejito a ver si estaba su dinero. Lo halló y se lo llevó a su casa.

Esa noche volvieron los muchachos por los cuatrocientos pesos y no hallaron nada. El viejito estaba cantando:

"Él que todo lo quiere
Todo lo pierde
Él que todo quiere
Todo lo pierde" ⸭

Pedro de Urdemalas

CUANTO HAY HABÍA una mujer que tenía tres hijos. El mayor se llamaba Manuel, el segundo Miguel, y el tercero se llamaba Pedro. A Pedro le decían todos "Pedro de Urdemalas" porque era muy travieso.

Como ya el papá había muerto cuando los hijos eran chiquitos, su madre no podía mantener bien a la familia. Los hijos sabían que tenían que salir a trabajar para mantenerse. Un día le dijo Manuel a su mamá:

—Mamá, voy a buscar trabajo con el rey para ganar reales para ti y para mis hermanos.

Todos sabían que este rey era muy malo y nadien aguantaba trabajar por él, de modo que nadien se sorprendió cuando Manuel nomás un día aguantó y luego volvió a su casa. Entonces Miguel, el hijo segundo, fue a trabajar por el rey y también no pudo aguantar más que un día y volvió a casa sin nada. Lo peor era que los hijos tenían lastimaduras en sus lomos de los azotes del rey. Todos estaban muy tristes, pues necesitaban ganar dinero, pero el siguiente día le dijo Pedro de Urdemalas a su mamá:

—Mamá, ahora me toca a mí ir a trabajar por el rey. Ahí verá el rey que con Pedro de Urdemalas no va a jugar.

Se fue caminando al castillo. Cuando Pedro llegó al palacio, lo primero que le dijo el rey fue:

—Te puedo dar trabajo tal como les di a tus hermanos, pero una cosa te voy a decir ahora mismo.

Tienes que obedecer mis órdenes sin cuestión ninguna. También ni yo ni tú podemos enfadarnos uno con el otro. El primero que se enfade le arrancará al otro tres tiras del lomo pero si me enfado yo, también te daré la mitad de mi reino.

Otro día le mandó el rey que llevara las vacas a pastar al monte. Cuando Pedro apenas había salido, vino el rey y le echó candado a la puerta del corral. En la tarde cuando volvió Pedro con las vacas, vido la puerta cerrada y se dio cuenta de que el rey estaba tratando de hacerle nojar. Pedro no se nojó, y como no podía cuestionar las órdenes del rey, tenía que figurar qué hacer. Por fin pensó en una idea y se puso a trabajar. Vino y degolló todas las vacas y las tiró para dentro del corral. Luego les cortó las piernas y las tiró y asina seguía.

Otro día se levantó el rey y fue a ver cómo había hecho Pedro para encerrar las vacas. Desatrancó la puerta del corral y se encontró con todas las vacas degolladas. Cuando vido esto, él escapó de reventar de coraje pero no lo mostró.

—Pedro, ¿Qué hicites con mis vacas? —dijo el rey.

—Pues, tuve que matarlas y echarlas en peso para encerrarlas dentro del cerco porque la puerta del corral estaba atrancada. ¿Se enfada por eso señor amito? —le preguntó Pedro.

—No me enfado, nomás digo —respondió el rey.

El rey pensó en cómo enfadar a Pedro de otro

modo y dijo:

—Oye Pedro, quiero decirte que aquí en el palacio llamamos por diferentes nombres algunas cosas. Por ejemplo, al gato llamamos "popurrate." Los calzones no llamamos calzones sino "childesbildres", y los zapatos llamamos "garabitates." A mí no me llaman rey sino "reverencia" y a la reina no llamamos reina sino "fordancia." También llamamos el castillo "petaca", la lumbre "clarencia" y el agua "paciencia." Quiero que de hoy en adelante uses estos nombres tú.

—Bueno, reverencia, no se me olvida — respondió Pedro. El rey pensó que Pedro iba a confundirse con esas palabras extrañas, pero Pedro era más vivo que el rey pensaba.

Cuando se llegó la noche y el rey y la reina se acostaron a dormir, vino Pedro y pescó al gato y lo envolvió en munchos trapos y le prendió lumbre, y lo echó en el cuarto donde estaba el rey y la reina. Pedro dijo en voz alta:

—Levántense su reverencia, también su fordancia. Pónganse sus childresbildres, también sus garabitates que aquí va el popurrate bien vestido de clarencia y si no cumplen con paciencia se les arderá la petaca.

Cuando el rey vido la lumbre se asustó muncho y le gritó a Pedro:

—¡Agua, Pelón!

—Paciencia, reverencia —respondió Pedro.

—Bueno, paciencia entonces, pero por favor haz lo que digo antes que se queme el palacio.

—Yo no sé de palacios, pero sí sé de petacas.

—Olvídate de los nombres que te dije y apúrate a apagar esta lumbre —le dijo el rey muy afligido.

Al fin apagó Pedro la lumbre y le preguntó al rey:

—¿Se enfada por eso, señor amito?

El rey quería gritarle a Pedro, pero obligado se vido a decir que no estaba nojado. Pensó en otro modo de enfadar a Pedro.

Otro día le dijo el rey que cercara la arbolera pero no le dio materiales para hacerlo. Pensó que por cierto eso le haría a Pedro enfadarse, pero Pedro dijo entre si mismo:

—Pues sin materiales para cercar me veré obligado a cortar los árboles para usarlos como postes.

Cortó todos los árboles y cuando acabó de cercar, fue a decirle al rey que viniera a ver. Fue a ver el rey y se encontró con todos sus árboles mochos.

—¿Por qué hicites esto? —preguntó el rey muy triste.

—Estuve obligado a hacerlo pues no me dio postes. ¿Se enfada por eso, señor amito?

—No, no me enfado, nomás digo —respondió el rey.

Ya el rey no hallaba qué hacer para hacer nojar a Pedro. Otro día, se fueron el rey y la reina a visitar otros reinos y llevaron a Pedro con ellos para que no hiciera nada mal mientras no estaban en la casa. Tenían que pararse en el camino una noche porque estaba muy lejos el reino que iban a visitar. Entonces le dijo el rey a Pedro que se fuera él adelante y que anunciara al rey y a la reina de ese reino que otro día llegaban ellos y que hiciera Pedro arreglos de posada y comida. Cuando le preguntaron a Pedro qué comida le gustaba a la reina, Pedro les dijo que su reina nomás poleadas comía.

Otro día cuando llegó el rey y la reina, los estaban esperando con un festín de poleadas. El rey y la reina no probaron bocado y notando esto la reina a quien visitaban les preguntó que si por qué no comían, siendo que les habían preparado su comida favorita. Pronto malició el rey que ésta era otra treta de Pedro para hacerlo nojar, entonces explicó que él y la reina estaban tan cansados de su viaje que no tenían hambre. Pidió permiso y se fueron con hambre a dormirse. Toda la noche el rey no dormía pensando en cómo hacerle a Pedro nojarse. Ya para la mañana tenía un plan.

Antes de ir a misa la siguiente mañana, el rey mandó a uno de sus sirvientes que fuera y le cortara la cola a la mula de Pedro. El rey tenía esperanzas que Pedro se enfadara cuando viera lo que habían hecho con su mulita. Pero cuando Pedro vido su mulita sin cola, pensó en su propio plan. Mientras estaban todos en misa vino Pedro y les cortó la jeta a todos los caballos del rey. Cuando salieron de misa, vieron a Pedro sentado fuera de la iglesia llorando.

—¿Por qué lloras, Pedro? ¿Estás nojado?— preguntó el rey.

—No, no estoy nojado. Estoy triste porque sus caballos se están riendo de mi mulita porque tiene la cola mocha —respondió Pedro.

Pronto fueron viendo el rey y la reina que todos sus caballos estaban desfigurados. Apenas podía controlarse el rey para no enfadarse, pero se quedó callado.

Ya el rey no sabía qué otra cosa hacer para desprenderse de este maldito Pedro. Estaba desesperado y decidió volver a su reino en vez de seguir en su viaje. Cuando iban de vuelta tuvieron que hacer campo junto a un río. El rey pensó:

—Esta noche echo a Pedro en el río y asina me desprendo de él para siempre.

Él le contó sus planes a la reina y en medio de la noche, fueron a ver si Pedro estaba dormido. Pedro estaba despierto porque él los había oído secretearse y malició lo que tenían intentado hacer. Estaba despierto cada vez que el rey y la reina vinieron a verlo. Se cansaron de esperar que se durmiera y se quedaron dormidos ellos. Entonces fue Pedro y con muncho cuidado agarró a la reina en brazos y la llevó para su cama. Y luego fue él y se acostó al lado del rey.

Muy de mañana, cuando todavía estaba oscuro, se despertó el rey y le dijo a Pedro, pensando que era la reina:

—Ahora sí parece que se durmió Pedro. Vamos a echarlo en el río.

Pedro no habló ni una palabra y se fue a ayudarle al rey a echar a la reina en el río. La miraban mientras se fue bajando el río. Cuando venían de vuelto le dijo el rey:

—Ahora sí vamos a vivir en paz sin ese Pedro de Urdemalas.

—Le está hablando a Pedro, señor amito —respondió Pedro.

Cuando vido el rey que había echado a su reina en el río en vez de a Pedro, se soltó llorando y dijo:

—Arráncame las tres tiras del lomo porque ahora sí estoy enfadado y triste. Tan pronto como lleguemos al palacio te daré la mitad de mi reino. ¡Que me dejes en paz!

Pedro volvió a su casa con muncho dinero y con la fortuna que ganó, vivieron muy contentos él, su mamá y sus dos hermanos la demás de su vida. ✛

Juan Rodajas

Cᴜᴀɴᴛᴏ ʜᴀʏ ʜᴀʙíᴀ un joven que llevaba por nombre Juan Rodajas porque en vez de andar como todos los hombres, rodaba como una rueda. Todos los días, iba por leña al monte y de vuelta venía rodando todo el camino con su carguita de leña.

Un día estaba Juan Rodajas en el monte cortando leña y luego que acabó se sentó debajo de un pino a comer. Cuando estaba comiendo su torta de pan, se le apareció un viejito y le dijo:

—¿Por qué no me das un pedazo de pan?

—Con muncho gusto —respondió Juan Rodajas muy pronto. Y partió el pan por la mera mitad y se lo dio al viejito.

—Tú eres un hombre muy bondadoso —le dijo el viejito—. Y por eso te voy a dar esta varita de virtud. Esta varita te da lo que tú pidas, si lo pides en la propia manera. Nomás le dices estas palabras: "Varita de virtud, por la virtud que tú tienes y que Dios te ha dado, haz que se me consiga este deseo."

Juan le dio gracias al viejito y su fue del monte rodando a su casa. Cuando Juan llegó a su casa, estaba muy cansado y con muncha hambre. Se recostó a descansar. Mientras descansaba estaba pensando qué iba a hacer de comer. Se acordó de la varita que le había dado el viejito. Agarró la varita de su bolsa y le dijo:

—Varita de virtud, por la virtud que tú tienes y que Dios te ha dado, haz que se ponga una mesa delante de mí con cuanta comida Dios creó.

Tan pronto como se le salieron esas palabras, se aprontó una mesa llena de muncha comida muy deliciosa. Como era un hombre pobre, nunca había visto tanta comida en toda su vida, y comió con muncho gusto de todo lo que estaba puesto delante de él.

Pasaba que el camino que Juan tomaba todos los días para el monte iba en frente del castillo del rey. Y un día cuando Juan venía rodando todo el camino con su carga de leña, estaba la princesa sentada en el balcón. Cuando vido a Juan pasar rodando, se soltó riendo. Juan sentía vergüenza y pensó:

—La princesa es muy orgullosa y se ríe de mí. Ya verá.

Cuando ya había pasado del castillo, sacó su varita de virtud de su bolsa y dijo:

—Varita de virtud por la virtud que tú tienes y que Dios te ha dado, haz que la princesa se ponga encinta sin saber.

La princesa ya no se reía cuando al cabo de nueve meses tuvo un niño. Como no estaba casada, el rey estaba muy enfadado con su hija y le mandó que le dijiera quién era el papá de ese niño.

—Te juro, papá, que yo no sé cómo me puse encinta —lloró la princesa.

Pero el rey no le creyó. Ordenó que todos los varones en su reino se aprontaran delante de él para ver quién era el papá del niño. Uno tras otro, vinieron los hombres delante de él. Pero el niño no se parecía a ninguno de ellos.

El rey estaba muy confundido y más nojado que nunca. Toda la noche anduvo alrededor del castillo encorajinado. Otro día vino uno de sus siervos y se hincó delante del trono y le dijo al rey:

—Su majestad, yo sé de un hombre que no se presentó delante de usted ayer. Su nombre es Juan Rodajas.

¡Juan Rodajas! —dijo el rey—. ¡No es posible que la princesa le hiciera caso a un hombre como Juan Rodajas.

Pero viendo que ya nomás a Juan faltaba llamar, despachó a uno de sus siervos que fuera por él.

Cuando llegó el siervo a su casa, Juan le dijo que sí iría a visitar al rey con muncho gusto. Se fue derecho, rodando hasta las meras puertas del castillo. Toda la gente lo vido y todos estaban asombrados que el rey llamara a Juan Rodajas.

Se abrieron las puertas del castillo y entró Juan. Ahí en el patio estaban el rey y la princesa con su niño. Tan pronto como vido a Juan, el niño empezó a gritar:

—¡Papá, papá!

La princesa se avergonzó muncho y le dijo al rey:

—¡No me diga que usted cree que Juan Rodajas es el padre de mi hijo!

Con muncho coraje le dijo el rey a su hija:

—Te tienes que salir de mi palacio hoy mismo. Has traído deshonra a mí y a toda mi familia. ¡Lleva a tu niño y vete con Juan Rodajas! No quiero verte nunca, jamás.

La pobre princesa salió del palacio llorando, siguiendo a Juan Rodajas, que rodaba todo el camino para su casa. La gente que estaba en el camino se reía y hablaba de ellos cuando iban pasando.

Otro día se despertó la princesa en la casa de Juan. Muy de mañana, se fue Juan por leña, y la princesa se quedó solita con su niño en el cuartito. Estaba ella acostumbrada a tener una criada que le ayudaba a hacer todo. No sabía vestirse sola, ni cocinar, ni darle de comer a su niño. Se puso a llorar de ver que no tenía nada de comida.

Esa noche cuando llegó Juan del monte, la princesa y el niño estaban dormidos. No habían comido en todo el día. Juan metió la mano en su bolsa y sacó la varita de virtud. Habló muy quedito para que no le oyera la princesa y dijo:

—Varita de virtud, por la virtud que tú tienes y que Dios te ha dado, haz que se ponga una mesa de comida de cuanto Dios creó.

Se apareció la mesa y él recordó a la princesa. Ella estaba sorprendida de ver tanta comida, pero estaba muy cansada para hacer preguntas. Los tres comieron a llenar, y luego comieron más. Ni en el palacio había comido la princesa tan buena comida.

Otro día pasó la misma cosa. Juan venía rodando a la casa e hizo que se apareciera comida mientras la princesa dormía. Pero esta vez la princesa abrió un ojo mientras pretendía estar dormida, y vido a Juan sacar la varita de su bolsa. Ella escuchó todas la palabras que él decía.

La siguiente noche la princesa esperó que Juan se durmiera y luego le quitó la varita. Otro día cuando Juan se fue al monte, ella le dijo a la varita:

—Varita de virtud, por la virtud que tú tienes y la que Dios te ha dado, haz que se aparezca una casa muy hermosa, amueblada con mejores muebles que los del rey, trajes de los más lujosos para mí, y vestidos para Juan. Y para mi niño, ropa como para un príncipe. —Ella pensó un momentito y al último de todo, le pidió que hiciera a Juan andar como todos los hombres en vez de rodando.

La varita de virtud le cumplió todo lo que ella le pidió. Esa noche Juan venía todo el camino andando en vez de rodando con la leña en el lomo.

—Ahí va Juan Rodajas, pero ya no anda rodando —dijieron los otros leñeros—. ¡Qué milagro!

La princesa y Juan se acostumbraron a vivir una vida muy buena. Cuando necesitaban alguna cosa, sacaban la varita, y todo les cumplía. Tenían la mejor ropa, una casa muy grande, y la mejor comida, y Juan ya no tenía que ir al monte a cortar leña.

La princesa estaba muy contenta y el niño pronto era un joven muy fino.

A poco tiempo la princesa decidió que era tiempo de invitar a su padre a comer con ellos. Cuando recibió la invitación, aceptó con muncho gusto, porque él había oído que había una casa en su reino tan hermosa como su castillo.

El rey fue para la casa con todos sus sirvientes. Cuando llegó, abrió la puerta Juan para recibir al rey, pero el rey no lo conoció porque traiba ropa muy elegante y ya no andaba rodando. La princesa también se compuso de tal modo que el rey no la conoció. Ella le había pedido a la varita que pusiera una mesa con la mejor comida del mundo.

En toda su vida, el rey nunca había comido tan buenas comidas. Él estaba muy sorprendido de ver a esta gente tan rica, porque él siempre había tenido más dinero que todos en el reino. El rey, Juan, la princesa y su niño comieron panes, carne, papas, y pastelitos de los más dulces del mundo.

Cuando ya habían acabado de comer, el rey y Juan se pusieron a platicar. Él le preguntó a Juan:

—¿Quién es tu padre que te ha dado tantas riquezas?

Juan le dijo los nombres de sus padres, pero el rey nunca había oído de esos nombres. No eran de la gente rica que vivía en su reino.

La princesa se fue para otro cuarto y le pidió a la varita, diciéndole:

—Varita de virtud, por la virtud que tú tienes y que Dios te ha dado, haz que se lleve el rey mi tumbaga de oro dentro de su zapato derecho.

Luego la princesa volvió al comedor y se estuvieron conversando hasta muy noche. Al fin el rey les dio las gracias por la comida tan buena y se fue con sus sirvientes y todos sus caballos. No hacía nada que había llegado el rey a su castillo cuando llegó un mensajero de la princesa.

—¿Qué se te ofrece? —le preguntó el rey—. Estoy muy cansado y necesito descansar.

—Mi ama me despachó a decirle que lo quiere ver tan pronto posible.

El rey no podía imaginar por qué lo quería ver la señora. Pensó:

—Posiblemente quieren decirme de dónde consiguieron tanta riqueza.

Cuando llegó a la casa de la princesa, ella le dijo:

—Gracias por volver, su majestad. Lo llamé para decirle que me falta mi tumbaga de oro. Y creo que usted se la llevó.

—¿Me estás acusando que soy ladrón? —exclamó el rey con coraje.

—Yo creo que trae mi tumbaga en su zapato —dijo la princesa.

—¡Mentiras! —dijo el rey—. ¿Y por qué quisiera yo su anillo y por qué lo escondería en mi zapato?

—Quítese el zapato del pie derecho y veremos —le mandó la princesa.

Cuando el rey se quitó el zapato, se le cayó la tumbaga en el suelo. El rey estaba espantado y le dijo a la princesa:

—¿Pero cómo es que yo traía esa tumbaga en mi zapato sin sentirla?

—Pues, ¿sabe quién soy yo? —le preguntó la princesa—. Pues, yo soy su hija a quien corrió usted de su palacio y asina como traía usted esa tumbaga de oro en su zapato sin sentirla, asina me puse yo encinta sin sentir.

Cuando el rey oyó todo esto, le pidió perdón a su hija, y le rogó que se fueran ella, Juan, y el niño a vivir con él en su castillo.

—Ya está perdonado —le dijo la princesa—. Munchas gracias por invitarnos a vivir con usted. Pero en nuestra casa estamos muy felices.

Y asina que su varita de virtud les dio a Juan, a la princesa, y al niño todo lo que deseaban en la vida. Nunca les faltó nada y vivieron felices el resto de su vida. ✢

Juan Sin Miedo

CUANTO HAY HABÍA un joven que se llamaba Juan. Desde que era chiquito, él no conocía el miedo. Mientras los otros niños se espantaban fácilmente y huían de cualquier ruido y de cada perro que ladraba, Juan nomás sonreía y seguía en su negocio.

—¿Por qué tanto miedo? —decía Juan. Por todo eso, su familia y toda la gente del pueblo le decía "Juan sin Miedo".

Un día cuando ya estaba joven, Juan le dijo a su mamá que se iba a ir a buscar trabajo. Se había muerto su papá trabajando en las minas y la familia tenía una vida muy dura.

—Ya es tiempo de salir a ganar dinero para tener una vida mejor —dijo Juan.

Su mamá no quería que Juan saliera, pero sabía que necesitaba comida y muebles para la casa, entonces lo dejó irse.

—Bueno —le dijo su madre—, vete a buscar trabajo afuera, pero ten muncho cuidado con los que andan procurando hacer mal en los caminos. ¿Me entiendes?

Juan oyó, pero no le importaban los consejos.

—¿Por qué tanto miedo? —dijo Juan, y recogió las pocas cosas que tenía para llevar en su viaje. Su mamá le preparó una gallina y galletas para el camino. Otros jóvenes también se fueron con Juan sin Miedo con el mismo fin—para ganar trabajo con el rey.

Caminaban todo el día y ya muy tarde, y cuando ya llegaba la noche, vieron una casa abandonada. Les dio miedo ver la casa, con las ventanas quebradas y el techo cayéndose. Algunos de los muchachos dijieron que sería mejor seguir en el camino hasta llegar a una casa donde vivía gente, pero Juan nomás encogió de hombros y les dijo:

—Pues ¿por qué tanto miedo? Pues ya es tarde, vamos a pasar la noche aquí.

Los otros dijieron que sí y caminaron hacia un portal de madera muy vieja. Rechinaba la puerta cuando la abrieron y salieron ratones voladores de las vigas, volando para afuera. Al fin los muchachos se acostaron en el suelo a dormir.

A poco rato oyeron muncho estrépito en el techo.

—¿Qué es eso? —gritaron algunos de ellos, corriendo para la puerta. Les dio tanto miedo que salieron corriendo. Pero Juan nomás los miró y dijo:

—¡Que no se apenen tanto! ¿Por qué tanto miedo?

Los muchachos tenían muncho respeto por Juan porque casi nunca se espantaba, y por eso volvieron y se pusieron sus cobijas y se acostaron otra vez en el suelo. Pero al momento que cerraron los ojos, empezó el estrépito en el techo, y esta vez también una voz quejándose. Al escuchar eso, los muchachos brincaron y se fueron huyendo. Juan se quedó solo diciendo:

—¿Por qué tanto miedo?

Luego se levantó y dijo:

—Tanto ruido me ha dado hambre —y sacó la gallina y las galletas y se puso a comer como si no pasara nada.

Mientras comía, oyó el estrépito en las latillas otra vez. Una voz muy triste decía:

—¡Caigo! ¡Caigo!

—O —dijo Juan, mirando las latillas—, cae, ¡pero no revuelques mi gallina!

Cayeron pedazos de las latillas con muncho polvo y luego cayó un hueso de pierna del techo y casi le pegó a Juan. Lo agarró Juan y lo tiró para un rincón con los huesos de gallina que había tirado, y siguió comiendo.

Más al rato empezó la voz otra vez diciendo:

—¡Caigo! ¡Caigo!

—¿Qué no puedes ver que estoy comiendo? ¡Cae, pero no revuelques mi gallina! —le volvió a decir Juan.

Cayó otro hueso de pierna del techo y lo agarró Juan y lo tiró para el mismo rincón donde había tirado el otro hueso. Siguió la voz diciendo la misma cosa y se cayeron luego los pies y luego los dedos, luego la cadera, y las costillas, y asina, con Juan respondiéndole la misma respuesta cada vez. Al fin se cayó la calavera, gritando —¡caigo! ¡caigo! — cuando cayó al suelo. Cuando Juan tiró la calavera junto los otros huesos, se formaron un esqueleto en el rincón. Juan lo vido y siguió comiendo su gallina y galleta como si nada pasara. El esqueleto miró a Juan un rato y luego le habló a Juan:

—Escarba ahí —dijo el esqueleto, apuntando al suelo con un hueso de dedo muy largo.

—¡O! —dijo Juan, mirando al esqueleto con coraje—, ¡cansado y muerto de andar y viene este amarilloso aquí a mandar!

—Escarba ahí —insistió el esqueleto.

—Bueno, en tal de que me dejes comer en paz haré lo que tú mandas.

Se puso a escarbar en el suelo. Al poco rato se dio con algo duro y cuando lo sacó de la tierra, halló que

era una tinaja. La limpió del polvo y la abrió y resultó que estaba llena de onzas de oro.

—Aquí tienes —le dijo Juan, dando la tinaja al esqueleto—. ¿Eso es lo que quieres? ¡Ahora tengo sueño y quiero dormir! ¡Que me dejes en paz!

Juan se puso su cobija y se acostó a dormir en el suelo. El esqueleto caminó hasta donde Juan estaba y dijo:

—Agarra este dinero. Yo quiero que pagues diez misas por mí para poder entrar el cielo, y el dinero que quede es tuyo.

—Bueno, pues. Como quieras —dijo Juan. Y puso la tinaja a su lado y durmió toda la noche sin apenarse y sin miedo de que el esqueleto estaba parado como sonriendo a su lado.

Otro día cuando recordó, Juan se fue a ver al cura del pueblo ahí muy cerca. Le dijo al cura:

—Me llamo Juan Sin Miedo y quiero pagar diez misas para el difunto que había muerto en tal casa que ahora está abandonada. Puedo pagarle ahora mismo.

Juan sacó la tinaja y le dio un manojo de onzas al cura. En ver tanto oro brillando, decidió el cura quedarse con toda la tinaja. Pensó en una manera de quitársela de Juan.

—Ven a este cuarto, amigo —le dijo el cura, y caminaron hasta que llegaron a un cuarto muy chiquito y sin ventanas. Abrió la puerta y cuando Juan entró, el cura cerró la puerta muy recio y la atrancó. A poco rato Juan se acostumbró a la oscuridad y miró todo lo que había en el cuarto. Había munchos esqueletos y calaveras en este cuarto. El cura pensó que encerrando a Juan en ese cuarto se iba a morir de puro miedo, y asina se quedaba él con todo el dinero.

Otro día fue el cura a ver si Juan se había muerto de miedo. Abrió la puerta y ¡lo halló jugando a la pelota con las calaveras!

—Agarra esta, padre —dijo Juan, y le tiró una calavera al cura. Brincó para atrás el cura y la calavera vino rodando hasta sus pies.

—Buenos días le dé Dios —dijo Juan, muy

respetuosamente—. Gracias por haberme dado este cuarto por la noche. Está muy suave.

Por fin el cura vido que no era muy fácil espantar a Juan y que no pudo quitarle el dinero.

—Ahora sí sé yo por qué lo llaman "Juan sin Miedo" —pensó el cura.

Le quedo dinero para diez misas nomás y le devolvió el resto a Juan. Le dio las diez misas para el alma del difunto que había vivido en la casa abandonada. Juan fue a cada misa y durmió cada noche en la casa abandonada. Sólo después de la última misa no dejó el esqueleto de gritar toda la noche y caminar para allí y para acá en el suelo.

Entonces se fue Juan para su casa. Se sorprendió su mamá de verlo en el camino después de tan poco tiempo afuera. Salió corriendo de la casa y le preguntó si había hallado trabajo.

—No, mamá —dijo Juan—. Ya no tengo que apenar más sobre el trabajo.

Le enseñó la tinaja de onzas a su mamá y le contó el cuento de todo lo que le había pasado.

—¿Pero qué vamos a hacer si ese dinero pertenece a alguien y viene a buscarlo? —preguntó su mamá, muy apenada—. ¿Y qué vamos a hacer si vuelve ese esqueleto a recogerlo?

—¿Por qué tanto miedo? —respondió Juan, y llamó a un carpintero y lo pagó con sus onzas de oro para levantar una casa muy hermosa para él y su madre. Y les quedó dinero para vivir toda la vida sin faltarles nada. ⊹

María Linda

Una vez había un hombre que tenía una hija que se llamaba María Linda. Este hombre era viudo y él y María Linda vivían solos.

Tenían una vecina que también era viuda y tenía una hija. María Linda iba a pasearse a casa de la vecina y la vecina era muy buena con ella. A María le gustaba visitarla porque cada vez que iba María Linda para su casa le daba sopitas con miel. Como María quería tanto a ella, un día le dijo María Linda a su papá:

—¿Por qué no se casa con la vecina? Ella es muy buena conmigo. Siempre que voy para su casa me da sopitas con miel.

El papá tenía que admitir que sí estaba muy solito. Hacía muncho que maliciaba que lo que quería la vecina era casarse con él, pero se preocupaba por su hija y cómo la trataría la vecina. Le dijo a María Linda:

—Hoy te da sopitas con miel, mañana te dará sopitas con hiel.

Pero María no le escuchaba y tanto molestó a su papá hasta que al fin se casó con la vecina.

Dicho y hecho, tan pronto como se casó el papá de María Linda con la vecina, empezó ella a maltratarla. María Linda tenía que hacer todo el negocio de la casa y su hija no hacía nada más que limpiarse las uñas y remudar túnicos todos los días. Con todo y andar hecha garras, María Linda era muy hermosa y la madrastra y la hija le tenían muncha envidia. Empezaron a planear cómo hacerle problemas.

María Linda tenía un borreguito que había criado desde que nació y un día nomás por hacerle mal a María Linda, le dijo la madrastra al papá que lo matara. A veces se mataba un borreguito y a todos les gustaba cordero asado de vez en cuando. Pero el papá no quería matarlo porque sabía qué tanto lo quería su hija, pero en tal de tener paz con su esposa hizo lo que ella mandó.

El papá mató el borreguito y lo preparó para asar. Guardó casi todas las partes del borreguito, aun las tripas que se usaban para hacer burriñates, una de las comidas favoritas de María. Despachó la madrastra a María Linda que fuera al río a lavar las tripitas. Se fue María Linda para el río llorando porque era tan cruel su madrastra. Cuando estaba lavando las tripitas se le fue una en el río. Mientras lloraba y miraba la tripa bajando el río, se le apareció una mujer vestida de azul con una corona de doce estrellas.

—¿Por qué lloras, linda? —le preguntó ella.

—Porque mataron mi borreguito y ahora se me fue una tripita en el río —respondió María Linda.

—No llores, yo la puedo recoger. Pero escucha. Allá en aquella casita hay un niño. Ve y míralo mientras yo busco la tripita —dijo la mujer.

Se fue María Linda para la casita y halló a un niño llorando y todo sucio. Había trastes puercos y ropa tirada por todas partes. Agarró al niño, lo limpió y lo puso a dormir. Después, limpió la casita y luego se fue para el río.

—¿Cómo estaba el niño? —le preguntó la mujer.

—Estaba llorando y todo sucio. Lo lavé y lo hice dormir y luego limpié la casita —dijo la joven.

—Aquí está la tripita que se te fue en el río y aquí está tu pago —le dijo la mujer, sonriendo.

Le tocó en la frente y le salió una estrella que brillaba como el sol.

Cuando llegó a la casa pronto le preguntaron que si cómo había resultado con esa estrella en la frente. Ella les contó todo lo que había pasado.

Cuando vido la hija la estrella le dio envidia y quería su propia estrella. Le pidió a su padrastro que matara a otro borreguito y se fue al río a lavar las tripitas, tanto como María había hecho. Mientras se sentaba cerca del río, lavando las tripitas en el agua, a propósito dejó caer una en el agua. Al mirarla desaparecer, pretendía que lloraba. A poco rato se le apareció la mujer vestida de azul y le dijo:

—¿Qué haces, joven?

—Se me fue una tripita en el río y ando buscándola —respondió la muchacha.

—Yo la buscaré. Curre a aquella casita donde hay un niño. Ve a ver cómo está.

Fue la muchacha y se encontró con el niño llorando y todo sucio. No le tenía paciencia con el niño y se puso enojada. Después de mirar la casa un poco, le dio nalgadas y lo dejó todo sucio, tal como estaba cuando llegó. Luego, volvió apriesa adonde estaba la mujer.

—¿Cómo estaba el niño? —le preguntó la mujer.

—O, estaba llorando y todo sucio. Le di nalgadas y lo dejé llorando —respondió la muchacha.

—Bueno, aquí está tu tripita y aquí está tu pago —le dijo la mujer.

Le pegó en la frente y le salió un cuerno. Se fue la muchacha para su casa muy contenta pensando que tenía una estrella como María Linda. Cuando la vido la mamá, se espantó muncho y también se enfadó porque ahora sí era más fea que nunca. Le dijo:

—¿Por qué es que tú vuelves con un cuerno en vez de una estrella como María Linda? ¿Qué no hicites lo mismo que hizo María Linda?

Cuando le platicó lo que había hecho ella, no pudo decir nada la mamá porque ella misma le había enseñado a ser egoísta y mala. Agarró un serruche la mamá y le cortó el cuerno pero tuvo que dejarle un pedazo para no herirle la frente. Para tapárselo se hacía caracoles en la frente.

Ahora eran más malas con María Linda. No la dejaban salir para ninguna parte porque era más hermosa que la hija especialmente ahora que tenía la estrella en la frente.

Poco después, aconteció que el rey iba a tener un baile para su hijo, el príncipe, para que conociera a las señoritas del reino y escogiera a una para ser su princesa.

Cuando llegó el día del baile, pasaron todo el día alistándose la madrastra y la hija. Compraron ropa muy fina y se estaban enfrente del espejo por horas y horas, arreglándose el cabello y componiéndose. Cuando se fueron al baile, dejaron a María Linda sola, limpiando la casa. Se puso María Linda a llorar y se le apareció la mujer vestida de azul. Le preguntó:

—¿Qué pasa? ¿Por qué estás llorando?

—Porque mi madrastra y su hija se fueron al baile que está dando el rey para el príncipe y no me convidaron —dijo María Linda.

—Por eso no te acongojes. Pide lo que quieras y yo te lo concedo.

María Linda le pidió un túnico de los más bonitos y unas chinelas color de oro. También pidió un coche y caballos para que la llevaran al baile. La mujer vestida de azul movió la mano y todas estas cosas se aparecieron. María Linda estaba tan contenta, subió en el coche y se fue para el palacio.

Tan pronto como llegó al palacio, el príncipe la vido. Le encantaron su sonrisa y la estrellita de oro en la frente. Pronto la sacó a bailar. El príncipe nomás con ella bailó toda la noche y mientras bailaban, empezó a hacerle munchas preguntas.

María Linda no quería decirle quién era porque sabía que su madrastra se iba nojar con ella. Cuando ya era muy noche, se dio una vuelta y se fue corriendo del baile y cuando iba saliendo, perdió una de sus chinelas. El príncipe se fue atrás de ella y pepenó la chinela.

Otro día salió el príncipe a buscar por todo el reino a la joven en quien le quedaba la chinela. Llegó a la casa de la madrastra y pronto salió la hija a medirse la chinela. Trataba de forzar el pie en la chinela, pero más que le forzaba, no le quedó. Muy triste dijo el príncipe:

—¿No hay nadien más que pueda medirse esta chinela?

—No —dijo la madrastra—, sólo tengo una hija.

En ese momento salió el gato de María Linda y empezó a gruñir y decía:

—¡Miao, miao! María Linda está en el estrao.

—¿Qué dijo ese gato? —preguntó el príncipe.

—O, no dijo nada —respondió la madrastra, dándole patadas al gato. Pero el gato gruñía más y más, diciendo:

—¡Miao, miao! María Linda está en el estrao.

El príncipe se agachó para oír al gato mejor, y por fin le entendió. Se sorprendió y dijo:

—¿Quién es esta María?

—Nomás es la criada. No le haga caso —respondió la madrastra.

—Pues, tráigala para acá para medirle la chinela a ella también —mandó el príncipe.

—Pero es fea y estoy cierta que no le va a quedar la chinela con los pies tan grandes. Tiene los pies llenos de callos de tanto trabajo, no como los pies bonitos de mi linda hija —dijo la madrastra.

El príncipe se puso sospechoso e insistió en ver a María Linda. Quiso que no quiso tuvo la madrastra que sacar a María Linda del estrado donde la tenían encerrada.

Salió María Linda y se puso la chinela y le quedó perfectamente. Luego sacó la compañera de la bolsa de su túnico donde la traía escondida y el príncipe vido que era la compañera de la chinela que se le cayó en el baile. Cuando le miró la cara, vido la estrella de oro en su frente. El príncipe le regañó a la madrastra por ser tan cruel diciendo:

—Usted ha escondido la belleza de esta joven por tanto tiempo, pero ¡ya no! Ya no va a estar escondida.

La llevó el príncipe con él al palacio. Ella insistió en que llevaran a su papá junto con ellos, pues él estaba tan triste de haberse casado con la madrastra. Poco después, se casaron. Hicieron festín y convidaron a toda la gente del reino, menos a la madrastra y a su hija. Después de la cena, tuvieron un baile y el príncipe y la princesa bailaron toda la noche. ✤

Los Tres Bueyecitos

CUANTO HAY VIVÍA UNA MUJER que tenía tres hijos y una hija. Llegó el día que tuvieron que salir los hijos a buscar su fortuna. Se quedaron la mamá y su hijita solas.

Pasó muncho tiempo y los hijos no volvían a la casa a ver a su mamá y a su hermana. Al fin se murió la mamá sin ver más a sus hijos y se quedó la hija sola. No halló más que hacer que irse a buscar a sus hermanos. Se fue caminando por munchos días hasta que al fin vido una casita en medio de unos jardines de maíz, calabacitas, repollo y otras verduras. Estaba cansada y tenía hambre, y esperaba meterse en la casita a descansar. Cuando llegó, tocó la puerta pero nadien respondió. Por fin abrió la puerta y entró y se asustó.

—Aquí parece que no hay mujer que limpie la casa. Todo está muy tirado —pensó la joven.

Se puso a poner todo en orden y luego su puso a preparar la cena. En la noche ella vido a tres jóvenes caminando hacia la casita, y ¡eran sus hermanos! Casi no lo podía creer, especialmente cuando voltearon y vinieron hacia la puerta de la casa.

—¡Qué suerte! Pero, ¿será que me van a reconocer? ¿Y estarán contentos de que yo esté en su casa? —pensó ella.

Para estar segura, la joven se fue a esconderse en un cuartito de atrás. Cuando llegaron los tres jóvenes, llevaron una gran sorpresa al hallar la casa limpia y la cena lista. Les dijo un joven a los otros:

—¿Quién habrá hecho todo esto por nosotros? Creo que hay alguien aquí.

Fueron buscando en todos los cuartos hasta que hallaron a la joven, pero no la reconocieron. Después de tantos años, ella ya era una joven bonita. Cuando la vieron tan hermosa y a solas, ellos se pusieron a discutir quién se casaba con ella. Luego se pusieron a platicar con ella y empezaban a reconocer ciertas cosas de ella.

—¿No vieron como ya sabía los nombres de cada uno de nosotros? —dijo el mayor—. Y miren, estas tortillas son iguales a las de mamá.

Poco después, descubrieron que era su hermana. Ella lo admitió y llevaron muncho gusto en estarse juntos otra vez.

—Ahora estamos juntos otra vez y estamos contentos —dijieron ellos.

Otro día los hermanos se preparaban para irse a trabajar otra vez muy temprano. Antes de irse, le encargaron a su hermanita que siempre tuviera la puerta atrancada porque tenían una vecina que era bruja.

—No debes ir a la casa de la vecina nunca, y siempre tienes que atrancar la puerta —le dijieron—, pues esa mujer es bruja y puede hacerte mal.

Todos los días los hombres iban a trabajar temprano y volvieron tarde y la hermanita limpiaba la casa y les hacía la cena.

Todo iba muy bien y estaban viviendo juntos muy felices hasta un día se apagó la lumbre y sin lumbre la joven no les podía hacer de cenar. No tenía más remedio que ir a pedirle brasas a la vieja bruja. Se puso su tápalo y salió para la casa de la bruja. Cuando iba en el camino, se encontró con unos muchachos.

Ellos le preguntaron:

—¿Para dónde vas, jovencita?

—Para esa casa para pedirle brasas a la bruja —les dijo.

—Esa vieja es muy mala y no te va a dar lumbre por su voluntad —le dijeron los muchachos—. Pero asómate en la puerta y si tiene los ojos abiertos, está dormida, y si están cerrados está despierta y no debes de entrar.

Se asomó la joven a la puerta y vido que tenía la bruja los ojos abiertos.

—¡Qué suerte! —pensó—. La bruja está dormida.

Entonces entró muy calladita y agarró unas brasas del fogón y salió corriendo. Pero en la salida trompezó en el marco de la puerta y recordó a la vieja bruja. Brincó la bruja y se fue atrás de la joven, pero la joven se fue corriendo muy recio y llegó a su casita antes de que le agarrara la bruja. Cerró la puerta y la atrancó. La bruja golpeaba la puerta para que le abriera, pero la joven no se atrevía hacerlo. Cuando vido la bruja que la joven no se la iba a abrir, se fue todo alrededor de la casa hablando y salpicando un líquido extraño, color de limón. En donde se caían las gotitas, salieron munchos coles de la tierra. La joven estaba mirando de la ventana, y luego comenzó la lumbre y se acostó a dormir. Ella se cansó con la corrida que echó para que no la pescara la bruja.

Esa noche cuando vinieron los hermanos del trabajo tocaban la puerta y su hermanita no les abría. Ellos traían muncha hambre y cuando vieron los coles, los cortaron y se pusieron a comerlos. Tan pronto como los comieron, se volvieron bueyecitos.

Cuando por fin se despertó la hermanita, se asomó a la ventana y vido a tres bueyecitos en un lado de la puerta. Ella pronto malició que la vieja bruja era la que había hecho esto con sus hermanitos. Se puso muy triste, pero de ese día en adelante, llevó la carga de cuidar a los bueyecitos como si fueran sus propios hermanitos. Todos los días los llevaba a beber agua del ojito y a comer zacate de la vega.

Un día iba el rey por el camino real y vido a la joven cuidando a sus bueyecitos en la vega. Como era tan linda, se enamoró el rey de ella. Se bajó de su caballo y se acercó a la joven. Hablaron un poco y pronto él le dijo que quería hacerla su reina.

—No —le respondió ella—. Yo no puedo casarme con usted, pues tengo que cuidar a mis bueyecitos.

—Yo entiendo —dijo el rey—, pero no se apene de sus bueyecitos. Si usted se casa conmigo, puede traer a sus bueyecitos con nosotros y tendrán el zacate más fino en todo el reino.

Se casaron el rey y la joven y ella fue a vivir con él en su palacio. Pero siguió cuidando a sus bueyecitos y estaba con ellos todos los días. Un día cuando los llevó al ojito a que bebieran agua, vido la joven a la vieja bruja que venía por agua. La joven subió un árbol para que la bruja no la viera. Cuando llegó la bruja al ojito, se agachó para llenar su cántaro de agua. Podía ver la imagen de la joven en el agua. Ella pensó que era su propia imagen que estaba viendo. Ella dijo:

—¡Yo tan linda y venir por agua! ¡Quiebro mi cántaro y me voy!

Tiró el cántaro y cuando dio la vuelta para irse miró para arriba y vido a la joven en el árbol. Se dio cuenta de que no era la imagen de ella que había visto en el agua sino la de la linda joven. A pesar de que fue su propia culpa, se enojó con la joven.

—Joven, bájate de ese árbol para que yo te vea mejor —dijo la bruja, muy suave.

La joven sabía que la bruja no tenía buenas intenciones y se estuvo en el árbol hasta que la bruja se cansó de esperar que se bajara, y se fue para su casa, murmurando que la iba a pescar algún día.

Todo estaba bien otra vez con el rey y su nueva

reina, pues vivían juntos muy contentos en el palacio y los bueyecitos en las vegas del rey. A poco tiempo tuvo la reina un niño. Lo cuidaba muy bien y con muncho cariño, pero no olvidaba de sus bueyecitos. Pronto quería hallar a alguien que cuidara a su niño mientras llevaba a sus bueyecitos a beber y comer en la vega. Asina que cuando la bruja supo de eso, vido la oportunidad de hacerle mal a la reina. Se compuso de tal manera que no la conociera la reina y fue al palacio y le dijo al rey que ella quería ser criada de la reina. El rey le dijo que sí podía tomar cargo de la reina y del niño.

Entró al cuarto donde estaba la reina con su niño y le dijo:

—Hijita mía, yo voy a tomar cuidado de ti. Déjame peinarte para que te veas muy hermosa para el rey.

Agarró el peine y mientras le peinaba le clavó un alfiler en la cabeza. Tan pronto como le clavó el alfiler, la reina se volvió una paloma y salió volando por la ventana. La bruja sonrió mientras miraba a la paloma volando y pronto cerró las cortinas para que el cuarto estuviera oscuro y se metió en la cama. Cuando entró el rey a dormir esa noche, la bruja le hablaba como si fuera la reina y dijo que no se sentía bien y que quería estar sola en el cuarto oscuro. El día siguiente le dijo lo mismo y el rey la dejó sola, pensando que estaba cansada de cuidar al niño.

Un día estaban los sirvientes del rey cortando trigo y voló la paloma cerca de ellos y se paró en un poste. Ella les dijo:

—¿Qué hace el rey con su negra mora? ¿A veces canta y a veces llora? ¿Y mis bueyecitos beben agua del ojito y comen zacate de la vega?

Pronto fueron los sirvientes y le dijeron al rey de lo que la paloma les había dicho. El rey les dijo que le trujieran la paloma tan pronto como la pudieran pescar. Fueron los hombres y pusieron trementina en el poste donde la paloma se había parado. A poco rato volvió la paloma y se paró en el poste. Se fueron los hombres por ella y cuando ella quiso volar no pudo por la trementina. Con cuidado se la llevaron al rey y él la agarró en la mano y se sentía familiar con ella. Se puso a alisarle la cabeza y a hablarle quedo. Mientras le tocaba la cabeza, encontró un tolondroncito y lo agarró y lo arrancó. Resultó que era el alfiler que la bruja le había clavado a la reina. Tan pronto como se lo arrancó, se volvió la paloma la reina en sus brazos. La reina le dijo que la mujer que estaba en su cama era la vieja bruja que había vuelto a ella una palomita y a sus hermanos unos bueyecitos.

El rey mandó a sus sirvientes que hicieran una lumbre con leña verde, que agarraran a la vieja bruja y que la echaran en la lumbre. Hicieron los sirvientes lo que el rey les mandó. Cuando estaba la bruja ardiendo, estaba con unas traqueaderas hasta que no quedó más que la ceniza. Tan pronto como se quemó, se volvieron los bueyecitos jóvenes otra vez. Se fueron a vivir con el rey y la reina y vivieron muy felices. ✛

El Caballero de la Pluma

UNA VEZ HABÍA UN HOMBRE y su esposa que no tenían familia. Ellos estaban muy tristes y todos los días le pedían a Dios que les mandara un hijo o una hija. Como dice el dicho, "Dios tarda pero no olvida," al fin les concedió su deseo y tuvieron un niño.

Cuando llegó el tiempo de bautizar al niño, convidaron a sus vecinos para padrinos. Estos vecinos eran muy pobres y no sabían qué llevarle a su hijado de regalo. Lo único que tenían para llevarle de regalo era un potrillo.

Cuando el niño tenía uso de razón, le dijeron sus padres que el potrillo era de él. No teniendo hermanitos ni hermanitas con quien jugar, él pasaba las horas con su potrillo. Llegó a tal grado que pasaba más tiempo con el potrillo que con sus padres. Munchas noches se iba a dormir con su potrillo. Siendo que era el único hijo que tenían, sus padres estaban muy tristes por todo lo que estaba pasando.

Una noche los oyó el joven secreteándose y le decía su papá a su mamá:

—Lo que debemos hacer es acabar con ese potrillo. La primera oportunidad que tenga, lo voy a hacer. Es la única manera de separarlos para poder ver a nuestro hijo.

Otro día fue el joven y le dijo a su potrillo lo que sus padres querían hacer con él. Le dijo el joven:

—Tenemos que salir huyendo esta misma noche. Mejor prefiero dejar a mis padres que estar sin ti.

El potrillo entendió todo lo que dijo el niño, pues en esos días los animales tenían virtud y podían entender y hablar como los hombres.

Le dijo al niño:

—Bueno, vamos a salir esta noche y te voy a llevar a un lugar seguro. Vamos al palacio del rey, y pueda que te dé trabajo. Pero te digo, vamos a pasar por lugares peligrosos. Debes quedarte en la silla y no atoques ni una cosa, no importa qué tal bonita sea. Si atocas algo, ¡tendremos mala suerte!

Salieron esa misma noche. Mientras caminaba el potrillo con el joven encima, el joven comenzó a tener sueño. Recordó muy de mañana cuando el sol apenas salía y vido que estaban en un lugar muy extraño que nunca había visto antes. Estaban pasando por un jardín muy verde con flores y árboles verdes y un río. Parecía que los árboles brillaban como el oro y que el agua brillaba como la plata. Pájaros de todos colores volaban entre los árboles cantando. El niño estaba encantado como si estuviera soñando.

—Este es un jardín encantado —dijo el potrillo—. Acuérdate de lo que te dije. ¡No atoques nada!

El joven miraba por todas partes con temor. Quería atocar los pájaros lindos tanto que cuando vido uno pasar, no podía resistir la tentación e hizo fuerza agarrarlo, pero el pájaro salió volando y solamente pudo agarrarle una pluma brillante.

—¡Ah, qué tonto! ¿No te encargué que no fueras a atocar nada? —le dijo el potrillo—. Ahora sí vas a tener mala suerte.

—¿Quieres que la tire? —le preguntó el joven.

—¡No! —le respondió el potrillo—. Si la tiras, te va peor.

El joven se puso la pluma en el sombrero y de allí en adelante toda la gente que lo vía le decía el Caballero de la Pluma. Siguieron su camino hasta que llegaron a un río muy grande con muncha lluvia. Tenían que cruzar para llegar al castillo del rey, pero no parecía que podían cruzar la primera corriente. Tenía miedo el joven, pero dijo el potrillo que no se apenara y que se prendiera bien para no caerse. Entraron al agua y el potrillo nadó con toda fuerza y el joven prendiéndose bien. Cuando llegaron al otro lado, ya no estaban en el jardín encantado. Todo era lo mismo como antes.

Al fin llegaron al castillo del rey. El joven entró y le pidió trabajo al rey y el rey le dio empleo. Después de un tiempo vido el rey que era muy buen trabajador y lo favorecía más que a los otros trabajadores que habían estado con él por más tiempo. Ellos envidiaron al Caballero de la Pluma e hicieron planes de hacerle un cuento al rey. Inventaron un cuento y fueron a ver al rey.

—Su majestad —le dijeron—, sabemos que su esposa, la reina, perdió la sortija de oro en el río hace muncho. El Caballero de la Pluma dice que puede sacarla del río.

Entonces el rey llamó al Caballero y le dijo:

—¿Es verdad que tú puedes sacar la sortija de oro de la reina del río?

—Nunca dije eso —respondió el joven. Se acordó de las aguas que había cruzado con el potrillo.

—Si lo dijiste o no, no me importa —respondió el rey—. Te mando que lo hagas hoy mismo o, si no, ¡pena de la vida!

El Caballero se fue muy triste a decirle a su potrillo lo que le había mandado el rey.

—Tú sabes que nunca podré sacar esa sortija de ese río tan fuerte —dijo el Caballero.

—Esta es la mala suerte que te está pasando porque agarrates esa pluma —respondió el potrillo—. Pero tengo una idea de cómo hacerlo.

El potrillo le habló por un buen rato y luego el joven salió corriendo. Fue a la plaza y compró papel de China. Cuando volvió al palacio, el rey le estaba esperando.

—Pues —dijo el rey—, estoy con ansias para que saques la sortija. Nos hace muncha falta por munchos años.

Mientras hablaba el rey, la gente del pueblo vinieron a ver lo que iba a pasar y sus compañeros del trabajo se secreteaban en voz baja que esto sería el fin del Caballero de la Pluma.

El joven se fue atrás del castillo a la orilla del río. Abrió la cajita de papel de China y ponía cada hoja, una por una, en el agua. Poco a poco el papel comenzaba a tragar el agua. Poco después, el río partió en donde estaba el papel y el Caballero de la Pluma entró en medio y pronto halló la sortija de la reina. Todos estaban asombrados y le aplaudían con alegría. El rey también se quedó sorprendido y le gustó lo que el joven había hecho, pero los trabajadores estaban nojados. Murmurando uno al otro, se prometieron inventar otro cuento.

Otro día, los trabajadores fueron a hablarle al rey y le dijeron:

—Sabemos que usted perdió su silla de marfil en un naufragio hace muncho. Ese Caballero de la Pluma dice que la puede sacar.

Otra vez lo llamó el rey y le dijo los rumores. El joven dijo que no podía hacer tal cosa pues había usado todo el papel de China en el pueblo. Pero el rey insistió, diciendo:

—Saca la silla de marfil del mar o, si no, ¡pena de la vida!

Cuando el joven le dijo al potrillo lo que había pasado, el potrillo meneaba la cabeza y se quedó callado por un tiempo. Por fin habló:

—Ve a la plaza y recoge todos los caballos que puedas hallar. Te venderán si les dices que yo te mandé. Cuando regreses, te diré mi plan.

Tan pronto como podía, el joven fue a la plaza y fue a todos los establos de todos los caballos. Los caballos relincharon cuando les dijo el joven las palabras que el potrillo le había dicho y saltaron los cercos de sus corrales para seguirlo. Cuando volvió al castillo, tenía miles y miles de caballos juntos con él. El potrillo les relinchaba cuando le pasaban los caballos, y todos hicieron una cola junto al mar. El joven no sabía qué hacer, pero su potrillo fiel le dijo:

—Ya les dije lo que tienen que hacer. Todo lo que tienes que hacer es pegar la pared del castillo con el azote tres veces y verás bien el camino a la silla.

El joven se quedó en frente del rey y de toda la gente que había venido de todas partes del reino, pues habían oído de la maravilla que había hecho el Caballero de la Pluma. El rey dijo:

—Pues, ¿puedes hallar la silla de marfil debajo de esas olas?

—Sí, puedo —dijo el joven, y pegó la pared tres veces con su azote de cuero. De una vez, los caballos se pararon de pies y saltaron en el mar, y cuando entraron, partieron las aguas del mar. Ahí en el fondo del mar, el Caballero de la Pluma vido la silla, media enterrada en el lodo. Pronto subió en su potrillo y salieron corriendo.

Cuando llegaba adonde estaba la silla, las aguas comenzaban a cerrar otra vez. Le quedaba poco tiempo, pero tiró una cuerda alrededor de la silla y el potrillo jaló fuerte. La silla salió del zoquete y corrieron hasta la tierra, tan pronto como las aguas cerraron.

Estaba el rey tan contento de tener otra vez su silla que lo hizo mayordomo de todos sus trabajadores. A pesar de que estaban nojados con el Caballero, ahora lo admiraban y estaban contentos de trabajar por él. El Caballero de la Pluma estaba muy agradecido de su potrillo y lo quería más que nunca, pero no se había olvidado de sus padres. Le pidió permiso al rey para traerlos al castillo y el rey con gusto le permitió ir por ellos. Salió en su potrillo cruzando el río por el jardín encantado. Esta vez tenía cuidado de no tocar nada. No agarraba a los pájaros lindos sino que los admiraba desde lejos. Se quedó encantado con los árboles brillantes, pero ya no quería llevarlos con él.

Cuando vieron los padres a su hijo, se soltaron llorando de gusto, diciendo:

—Perdona que queríamos acabar con ese potrillo. Nomás queríamos tener más tiempo contigo.

El Caballero de la Pluma les dijo que los perdonó y les dijo de sus aventuras con el potrillo. Los padres se quedaron asombrados con el potrillo y todo lo que podía hacer.

—Nunca sabíamos que tenía virtud —dijieron.

El Caballero de la Pluma y sus padres ensillaron a sus caballos y todos fueron al castillo donde el rey les dio cuartos muy grandes, ropa fina y toda la comida que podían comer. Ahí vivieron el resto de sus vidas, El Caballero de la Pluma, sus padres y el potrillo fino. ✛

María Bernarda

UNA VEZ HABÍA UNA DONCELLA que se llamaba María Bernarda. Ella tenía una mulita que se había criado con ella y ella y esta mulita se querían muncho. Eran tan buenas amigas que podían hablarse una a la otra, como la gente. Hace muncho tiempo la gente podía hacer eso y los animales tenían virtud.

Bueno, pues, María era muy hermosa pero también muy orgullosa. Munchos jóvenes venían a pedirle la mano pero no quería casarse con ninguno de ellos. Ella decía:

—Yo no me caso hasta que no venga a pedirme uno que tenga dientes de oro y barbas de plata.

El diablo se dio cuenta de lo que María Bernarda decía y se puso con unos dientes de oro y una barba de plata y fue a pedirla. Cuando lo vido María Bernarda con dientes de oro y barbas de plata pronto le dijo que sí se casaba con él. Mure tonta, ella pensaba que era el hombre a quien esperaba.

María fue a decirle a su mulita que por fin había conocido al hombre con quien se casaba. Pero en vez de estar contenta, la mulita se puso muy triste porque sabía que el hombre con los dientes de oro y la barba de plata era el malo. Le dijo:

—¡Ah, qué muchita! Él que tú has escogido para ser tu marido no es otro más que el diablo.

—¿Es cierto? ¡No me digas! ¿Qué voy a hacer hora? —preguntó María Bernarda, muy acongojada.

—Pues dile que tú no sales de tu casa sin tu mulita y lleva siempre tu escapulario. Yo te aviso de sus engaños y el escapulario te cuidará de él —dijo la mula.

—Bueno, amiguita, —le dijo María Bernarda—, mi escapulario no me lo quito yo, y yo me quedo cerquita de mi mulita.

El diablo se subió en su caballo y ella en su mulita. Partieron para la casa del diablo muy lejos. No habían caminado muncho cuando llegaron a un río de sangre. Pararon a mirar el río horrible. María no sabía cómo iban a pasar.

—No te preocupes —dijo la mulita—. Dile al diablo que tú pasas primero y todo va a estar bien, pero acuérdate de prenderte bien y lleva el escapulario.

María le dijo al diablo que ella entraría primero, y agarrando bien a su mulita con una mano y su escapulario con la otra, entraron al río. En ese momento, el río se abrió y las dejó pasar sin que las tocara ni una gota de sangre. Luego las siguió el diablo, pero cuando comenzó a cruzar, se juntó el río de sangre y él y su caballo llegaron a la otra orilla todo ensangrentados. El caballo pataleó para quitarse la sangre, y el diablo hacía una cara fea. María vido que ya no brillaban tanto sus dientes de oro ni su barba de plata.

Poco después, seguían caminando un largo trecho hasta que llegaron a un río de estillas. La mulita otra vez entró primero con María Bernarda y se abrió el río de estillas y las dejó pasar. Cuando el diablo

quiso cruzar el río, se juntaron las estillas y lo clavaron por todo el cuerpo. Él gritó y su caballo se paró de pies, pero sí llegaron al otro lado. El diablo miró a María muy feo, pero no le dijo nada.

Comenzaron a caminar otra vez hacia la casa del diablo, pero pronto llegaron a otro río. Este río era pura lumbre y casi los quemaba al acercarse. María tenía miedo, pero tenía confianza en su mulita y su escapulario. Cerró los ojos y agarró su escapulario cuando la mulita entró al río. De repente, la lumbre se dividió e hizo un camino para la mulita y María Bernarda y pasaron sin contingencia. Luego le tocó al diablo entrar. Sonrió, pues ya estaba acostumbrado a la lumbre y al calor, sabes, y no pensaba que podía quemarse. Pero cuando el diablo quiso pasar, se juntó el río de lumbre y pasó pero todo quemado. Ya estaba muy nojado para hablar y sus dientes de oro y su barba de plata estaban negros del humo.

Ya estaban acercándose a la casa del diablo y María comenzó a tener miedo, pues si llegaron a su casa, tendría que vivir con el diablo por toda la vida. Pensó en cuántas veces había rechazado a tantos hombres finos.

—Tuve tantas oportunidades para casarme, pero me sentía mejor que todos —pensó ella—. Si salgo de esto, ¡nunca quiero casarme con nadien!

Fueron caminando hasta que llegaron al último río antes de la casa del diablo. Ahí estaba un río de navajas. Podían ver la casa del diablo al otro lado. Ya por la última vez, la mulita y María entraron, María con los ojos cerrados y apretando bien su escapulario. De repente, el río de navajas se abrió y las dejó pasar. Pronto entró el diablo siguiendo muy cerquita para no tocar las navajas, pero cuando su caballo entró se juntaron las navajas y cortaron al diablo en todo el cuerpo. Cuando llegó a la otra orilla, cayó muerto.

—María Santísima te ha estado cuidando —dijo la mulita—. Ahora seguiremos caminando a ver qué suerte encontramos.

María estaba contenta de estar libre del diablo, pero juró que nunca se casaría otra vez. Salieron troteando sin saber qué les esperaba más adelante.

Poco después, llegaron adonde estaban unos pastores cuidando a sus ovejas. María tuvo una idea para que nadien más le pidiera la mano. Les pidió traje de hombre y le ofrecieron ropa vieja y rasgada. María se puso la ropa, subió en su mulita y siguieron caminando.

Unos días después, llegaron al palacio del rey. María quería muncho vivir ahí, pues era un lugar tan bonito. Le dijo al rey que se llamaba Bernardo y que andaba buscando trabajo. El rey le dio empleo.

El rey tenía un hijo que siempre estaba triste y nunca hablaba ninguna palabra. Todos los días se sentaba en el balcón, mirando a la gente que pasaba. Un día estaba sentado en el balcón y vido a María Bernarda. Él dijo:

—Miren qué mancebo va ahí.

Todos se sorprendieron que el príncipe hablara. El rey y la reina llevaron tanto gusto que el príncipe habló que llamaron a "Bernardo" y le dijieron que de esa hora en adelante querían que fuera el compañero constante del príncipe. Asina que todos los días platicaba con el príncipe y se paseaban por los jardines del castillo. Entre más días se alegraba el príncipe más y más y le estaba agarrando más voluntad a "Bernardo."

Un día le dijo el príncipe a la reina:

—¿Sabes qué? Se me hace que los ojos de mi amigo "Bernardo" Bernardita son!

—¿Por qué dices eso si es hombre, hijo? Pero para desengañarnos, mañana le diré a uno de los sirvientes que lo lleve para el jardín y si le gustan las flores es seña que "Bernardo" no es "Bernardo" sino Bernardita.

La mulita escuchaba todo lo que decían y fue y le dijo a María Bernarda sus planes. El siguiente día le dijo el sirviente:

—Vamos a ver el jardín.

—O no, gracias. Yo no estoy interesado en flores —respondió María Bernarda—. Nomás las mujeres se interesan en eso.

Pronto volvió el sirviente a la reina.

—¿Cómo le gustaron las flores a "Bernardo"? —le preguntó la reina.

—Ni quiso ir al jardín. Me dijo que a él no le interesaban las flores —dijo el sirviente.

Fue la reina y le dijo al príncipe:

—Tu amigo "Bernardo" es hombre. No le gustan las flores.

—O no, todavía se me hace que los ojos de "Bernardo" Bernardita son —dijo el príncipe.

—Bueno —dijo la reina—, mañana lo convidas a andar a caballo y le das el caballo más rejiego. Si lo maneja bien, sabremos que es hombre, pero si no, sabremos que es Bernardita.

La mulita estaba debajo de la ventana de la reina comiendo zacate y escuchó su plática. Otra vez fue la mulita y le dijo a María Bernarda los planes que ellos tenían.

—¿Qué voy a hacer esta vez, amiguita? Sólo sé pasearme en ti, mi mulita —dijo María Bernarda.

—No vayas a usar la silla que te den ellos; usa la mía —le encargó la mulita—. Asina vas a pensar que estás conmigo.

Otro día fueron al corral y el sirviente escogió un caballo muy rejiego.

— Bernardo, mi amigo, aquí está tu caballo —dijo el príncipe.

Ella le dijo:

—Está bien, pero yo nunca uso una silla más que la de mi mulita.

—Está bien —dijo el príncipe, y le puso la silla de la mulita en el caballo rejiego.

Cuando se sentó en la silla de su mulita, el caballo se quedó manso. Fueron a los campos a pasear y María salió mejor jinete que el príncipe. Pero todavía el príncipe no estaba convencido que su amigo "Bernardo" era hombre. Después se fue al castillo a contarle a la reina de su paseo.

—Pues, es difícil convencerte, pero tengo más una prueba. Esta noche —dijo la reina—, despacharemos a uno de los sirvientes a mirar a Bernardo mientras esté durmiendo. Sin su sombrero sabremos si es hombre o mujer.

Esta vez la mulita estaba en el corral comiendo zacate y no oyó la conversación entre el príncipe y la reina. Pensaba, junto con María, que por fin le habían convencido al príncipe que ella era hombre. Pero esa noche, el sirviente entró en su cuarto a ver a "Bernardo" mientras dormía y vido que tenía cabello que le llegaba a la cintura. Pronto fue y le dijo a la reina lo que había visto. En la mañana la reina fue a decirle al príncipe:

—Pues, es verdad, hijo. Ve a decirle a tu amiga que sabemos su secreto. Tal vez nos diga quién es.

Cuando el príncipe oyó esto, pronto fue y le dijo:

—¡Hemos descubierto tu secreto, Bernardo! Siempre maliciaba que eras mujer, y me enamoré de ti. Ahora sé que esos ojos son de Bernardita y la única cosa que quiero para estar feliz en este mundo es que tú seas mi princesa.

Muy asustada porque descubrieron su secreto, María miró a su mulita. La mulita se bajó las orejas y le dijo:

—Pues, supongo que no podíamos guardar el secreto para siempre. Creo que debes casarte con este joven fino.

María Bernarda consintió casarse con él, pero sólo si podían traer a la mulita a vivir con ellos. El príncipe dijo que sí, y desde entonces vivieron muy felices el príncipe, María Bernarda y la mulita junto con ellos. ✣

El Pastorcillo

Había una vez un joven que era borreguero. Todos los días él se iba para el monte a cuidar sus borregas. Siempre prendía una lumbre para cocinar su comida y calentarse por la noche. Estaba muy contento en el monte con sus borregas.

Un día prendió una lumbre cerca de muncha rama seca y de repente se prendieron las ramas. El pastorcillo corrió y agarró una cobija. Estaba tratando de apagar el fuego cuando vido una viborita que estaba queriendo salir de la lumbre y no podía. El pastorcillo sintió lástima por el animal y agarró un palo y sacó la viborita del fuego.

La viborita estaba muy agradecida del pastorcillo porque le había salvado la vida. Le dijo al pastorcillo:

—Como has sido tan bondadoso conmigo te voy a llevar a mi padre, el viborón. Él es muy poderoso y quiero que le pidas una dádiva. Pero una cosa te aconsejo: No le vayas a pedir riquezas ni cosas asina porque tal cosa le enfada y te puede matar. Nomás dile que quieres entender el idioma de todos los animales. Él no va a convenir pronto, pero siempre dile que nomás eso quieres.

Caminaron por las montañas hasta que llegaron adonde estaba el viborón debajo de una piedra grande y redonda. Cuando vido al hombre viniendo con su hija, parecía de mal humor y sacó la lengua. El hombre y la viborita llegaron a hablarle y le dijo la viborita lo que el pastorcillo había hecho.

—Como me ha salvado la vida quiero que le otorgue una merced —pidió la viborita.

—Bueno —dijo el viborón—. ¿Qué es lo que quieres?

—Pues, quiero entender el idioma de todos los animales —respondió el pastorcillo.

El viborón se retiró y dijo:

—Pide otra cosa.

—No —le dijo el pastorcillo—. Nomás eso quiero.

Después de un rato le dijo el viborón:

—Bueno, pues te voy a otorgar esta merced. Pero te digo, el día que tú le digas a otra persona que entiendes el lenguaje de los animales, ¡te morirás!

Se fue el pastorcillo de vuelta a cuidar sus ovejas y se sentó abajo de un pinabete. Estaba pensando de qué le servía entender el idioma de los animales cuando dos cuervos vinieron y se sentaron en el mismo pinabete. Cuando empezaron a caracaquear uno al otro, como hacen los cuervos, el pastorcillo les entendió. Uno le decía al otro:

—¡Qué tal si este pastorcillo supiera que debajo de este pinabete está un tesoro enterrado!

—Se hacía rico —respondió el otro—. Pero nunca lo va a saber. —Los dos comenzaron a reírse y se volaron, caracaqueando.

Pronto se puso a escarbar el pastorcillo hasta que encontró una tinaja colmado de onzas de oro. Con todo este dinero se hizo un hombre muy rico y ya no tuvo que trabajar cuidando a borregas.

—Ahora voy a tener una casa y me voy a casar con una mujer buena —dijo el pastorcillo.

Entonces, el pastorcillo salió del monte y levantó una casa en el valle. Luego se casó con una mujer bonita. Al comienzo, el pastorcillo extrañaba el monte y sus ovejitas, pero pronto se puso contento con su mujer y los animales que tenía en el corral.

Un día iban a pasearse en caballo él y su esposa que estaba encinta. Él se subió en el caballo y ella en la yegua. Cuando iban en el camino, relinchó el caballo y le habló a la yegua. Como el pastorcillo entendía el idioma, le entendió lo que le dijo.

—¡Anda más apriesa, perezosa! —le dijo el caballo a la yegua.

Ella levantó las orejas y abrió la boca con una risita. La mujer no se dio cuenta del ruido que hacía la yegua, pero el pastorcillo le entendió lo que decía:

—Sí —respondió la yegua—, como tú llevas uno y yo llevo dos.

Cuando el pastorcillo oyó lo que le dijo la yegua al caballo, soltó la carcajada y siguió riendo todo el camino.

—¡Mi mujer está encinta y vamos a tener un hijo! —pensaba él.

Su mujer lo miró y le dijo:

—¿Por qué te ríes tanto?

—O, nomás porque me dieron ganas de reírme —respondió el pastorcillo.

—Me tienes que decir por qué te ríes —dijo la mujer.

—O, no puedo decirte —respondió el pastorcillo.

—¡Tienes que decirme por qué te ríes! ¿De qué estabas pensando que te hizo reír? ¿Me veo chistosa?

Poco después, el hombre se cansó y se voltearon para volver a casa. En todo el camino le molestaba la mujer a su esposo. Trataba él de decirle cosas para que se le olvidara del asunto, pero se ponía más y más nojada, insistiéndole que le dijiera.

Entraron a su casa y todavía siguió preguntándole. Tanto lo mortificó al pobre hombre que en tal de que callara la boca y lo dejara en paz, pensó decirle por qué se había reído tanto, a pesar de que el viborón le había dicho que no dijiera su secreto a nadien.

Otro día se levantó muy de mañana y se puso a hacer su cajón de entierro. En la tarde acabó y se sentó afuera a descansar. Estaba él muy triste porque sabía lo que iba a pasar. Mirando los animales en los establos, extrañaba los días cuando estaba libre en el monte. Ahora sentía angustia de haber encontrado esa víbora en la lumbre.

El perro estaba echado junto a su amo y le dijo al gallo que andaba ahí:

—¿Por qué andas tan contento? ¿Qué no sabes que nuestro amo se va a morir?

—¡Que se muera! —dijo el gallo—. ¿Por qué es tan tonto? Yo cuando hallo un grano de maíz llamo a las gallinas y antes de que ellas lleguen me lo como.

El hombre escuchaba lo que el gallo estaba diciendo y dijo:

—Dice bien el gallo. ¡Qué tonto soy yo! No tengo que decirle todo a mi mujer. —Pronto volvió a casa y halló a su mujer en la cocina.

—¿Me vas a decir por qué estabas riendo? —le preguntó.

—No, no te voy a decir nada —dijo el pastorcillo—, y ¡debes de parar de molestarme y entonces podemos vivir en paz!

Fue y la encerró en un cuarto y le dijo que no la iba a dejar salir de ahí hasta que no dejara de mortificarlo. Cuando vido la mujer que su esposo no iba a hacer lo que ella decía, prometió que no le decía más nada de la risa ni de lo que estaba pensando él.

En pocos meses, la mujer dio a luz a un hijo. Él hombre se rió, pues sabía todo ese tiempo que estaba encinta. Mientras tenía el niño en su rodilla, pensó:

—Ahora si pudiera entender el idioma de los niños.

Nunca supo nadien el secreto del pastorcillo. Munchas veces los animales le ayudaron y él y su esposa vivieron una vida larga y feliz. ✛

Juan Tonto

CUANTO HAY VIVÍA una mujer que tenía un hijo que se llamaba Juan. Todos lo llamaban Juan Tonto porque siempre hacía cosas tontas. Una mañana cuando todavía estaba Juan roncando, le habló su mamá:

—Juan, levántate a ver si hay lumbre.

Juan llamó al gato y lo tocó y dijo:

—Sí, hay lumbre, nana. El gato todavía se siente caliente.

La pobre mujer quería que Juan se levantara a hacer algo por la vida. Le dijo:

—Juan, levántate a ver si llovió anoche.

Pero en vez de levantarse, Juan llamó al perro:

—¡Chito, chito, chito! —Entró el perro y lo tocó. Luego le dijo a su mamá:

—Sí llovió anoche, nana. El perro está mojado.

Tratando otra vez de hacerle levantarse, la mamá le dijo:

—¿Sabes qué Juan? Ya tu vecino se levantó y se halló un talegón de dinero.

—Pero nana, más de mañana se levantó él que lo perdió —le contestó Juan.

—Válgame Dios, Juan —dijo su mamá—, tengo que ir a trabajar para ganar con qué comprar comida. Tú eres tan flojo que si me aguardo a que tú hagas algo nos muremos de hambre. Aquí te encargo al niño mientras voy a buscar trabajo.

—Bueno, nana, váyase a buscar trabajo —respondió Juan, muy flojo para levantarse.

Al rato que se fue empezó el niño a llorar. Pero Juan estaba demasiado flojo para levantarse y cuidarlo y el niño seguía llorando. Por fin Juan gritó:

—O, ¡cállate el hocico! —Y le tiró uno de sus zapatos al niño. El niño se calló y Juan pensó:

—Ahora sí que le enseñé algo. ¿Por qué no le muestra mi nana quién manda asina como yo?

Más tarde ese día la mamá volvió y le preguntó:

—¿Cómo está el niño?

—O —dijo Juan—, lloró un rato, pero yo le enseñé quién es el que manda y ha estado durmiendo todo el día.

Fue a ver la mamá a su hijito y fue viendo que Juan lo había golpeado con su zapato y estaba en desmayo. Tenía una lastimadura en la cabeza.

—¿Qué fuiste hacer con mi hijito? —dijo la mamá muy afligida—. Voy a tener que dejarlo con su abuela. Ahora me voy de aquí para nunca más volver. Ahí te encargo la puerta para que nadien entre.

Se fue la pobre mujer y se quedó Juan Tonto solo.

—¿Qué voy a hacer sin mi nana? —pensó Juan.

No aguantaba estarse solo, entonces quitó la puerta y se la echó en el lomo y se fue en pues de su nana. Ya muy tarde la alcanzó. Cuando vido su mamá que le había seguido se le cayó el cielo encima y le dijo:

—Juan, ¿para qué me fuites a seguir y por qué traes la puerta contigo? —No podía creer que él la

había seguido.

—Pues, nana, ¿Qué iba a hacer yo solito en la casa? ¿Y no me encargates la puerta? Por eso la truje conmigo —respondió Juan.

—Dios mío, ¿ya qué puedo hacer? Nomás sufrir lo que me toque —dijo la pobre mamá.

Habían caminado un largo trecho cuando vieron venir en la distancia munchos hombres a caballo. Dijo la mamá:

—Tantos hombres a caballo tan lejos de todo. No han de tener buen fin, Juan. Vamos a subirnos aquel árbol para que no se den cuenta de nosotros.

La mamá subió el árbol y Juan la siguió con la puerta cargada. No hacía nada que habían acabado de subir cuando llegó la pandilla de hombres. Eran unos ladrones y traían munchos sacos llenos de dinero. Se pusieron a hacer de cenar abajo del árbol en donde estaban Juan y su mamá.

Estaban contando todos los robos que habían hecho y qué tanto dinero tenían ya escondido en la casita ahí cerquita. Mientras ellos platicaban, Juan y su mamá escuchaban todo lo que decían.

A poco rato, Juan le dijo a su mamá en voz baja:

—Nana, ¡ya mero me meo!

—¡Por favor de Dios, aguanta, Juan!

Poco después, Juan dijo otra vez:

—Nana, ¡ya mero me meo!

—¡Aguanta, Juan, aguanta! —le insistió la mamá.

Juan hizo fuerza aguantarlo pero no pudo, entonces se quitó la mamá su bota y dijo:

—Méate en esta.

Juan trató de mear en la bota, pero se les cayeron unas gotas en los ladrones. Uno de ellos miró para arriba y Juan y su mamá pensaban que por cierto los habían visto.

—¡Ah, qué pájaros tan cochinos! —gritó el ladrón. No vido a Juan ni a su mamá entre las ramas.

Poco después, Juan le dijo:

—Nana, ¡ya mero me cago!

—¡No me digas eso, Juan! Nos van a descubrir y por cierto nos matan. ¡Aguántalo!

—No puedo, nana —le dijo.

—Bueno, Juan, ¡cállate y toma mi bota!

Juan trató de pasar en la bota, pero se les cayó poco en los ladrones.

—¡Ay! ¡Qué pájaros tan cochinos! —dijo uno de ellos, mirando hacia arriba—. Si no paran, les voy a dar un balazo.

Los hombres seguían hablando y fumando y Juan y su nana pensaban que ya no estaban en peligro, pero ya se cansaban de estar en el árbol. A poco rato, Juan le dijo a su mamá en voz queda:

—Nana, esta puerta está muy pesada. ¡Ya mero la suelto!

—Por favor de Dios, Juan, ¡no la sueltes! —le dijo la mamá.

—¡No puedo, nana! —dijo Juan y antes de que pudiera contestarle su mamá, la soltó y se fue cayendo la puerta quebrando las ramas.

Se sorprendieron los ladrones y miraron para arriba para ver de dónde venía tanto ruido. Uno de ellos vido a Juan y a su mamá, pero cuando quiso gritar, se le cayó la puerta en la mera boca y se le partió la lengua en dos. El ladrón quiso decirles a los otros que había gente en el árbol, pero en vez de palabras se le salieron tonterías:

—¡Biliabila bilia brilit! —decía.

Se espantaron sus amigos y salieron huyendo, con su amigo corriendo atrás, gritando tonterías. Dejaron a todos sus caballos y los sacos de dinero.

Esperaron un rato para ver si volvían los ladrones y cuando vieron Juan Tonto y su mamá que ya no volvían se bajaron del árbol y agarraron los sacos de dinero.

Otro día se levantó Juan muy de mañana y fue a buscar trabajadores para que le ayudaran a levantar una casa. Pues ahora que se vido Juan con tanto dinero hasta lo flojo y lo tonto se le quitaron. Cuando vido la gente que Juan estaba levantando casa, pronto fueron y le dijieron al rey, pues nadien creía que Juan fuera tan vivo ni que tuviera el dinero para levantar una casa. Le dijieron al rey que la casa de Juan sería más bonita que el castillo del rey.

—Pero ¿cómo? —dijo el rey—. No puede ser que

ese Juan Tonto tenga tantos reales.

Pronto mandó a dos de sus criados que fueran a llamar a Juan. Cuando llegó Juan, el rey le preguntó:

—Pues ¿Cómo te hicites tan rico de la noche a la mañana? No eres él a quien le llaman "Juan Tonto"?

—Pues sí, soy yo mismo —le respondió Juan—. Y lo hice robando.

—Pues ¿que eres ladrón? —le preguntó el rey.

—¡Y ladrón fino! —dijo Juan.

—Bueno —le dijo el rey—. Esta noche quiero que me robes la sábana donde yo duermo. Y si lo haces no sólo creo que eres ladrón fino sino que también te daré la mitad de mi dinero. Y si no puedes, ¡pena de la vida!

Fue Juan para su casa e hizo un muñeco de la figura de él y le puso una cuerda. Cuando se llegó la noche, fue para el palacio del rey y puso el muñeco cerca de la ventana donde dormían el rey y la reina. Ellos estaban despiertos esperando que Juan viniera a robarles la sábana. Cuando el rey vido el bulto cerca de su ventana, le dijo a la reina:

—Ahí está Juan. ¡Voy a correrlo!

El rey salió para fuera y Juan le jaló la cuerda al muñeco y salió el muñeco corriendo, y el rey atrás de él. En esto entró Juan al cuarto y le dijo a la reina:

—¡Esconde la sábana en la petaquilla que está en el zaguán para que no la halle Juan!

Al rato llegó el rey y le dijo a la reina:

—Ya corrí a Juan.

—¿Pues que no entrates tú ahorita y me dijites que escondiera la sábana en la petaquilla? —dijo la reina, bien confundida.

—No fui yo —le respondió el rey—. Ya Juan nos jugó una treta.

Otro día fue Juan a entregarle la sábana y le dijo el rey:

—Este robo no cuenta. Tú me jugates una treta. Esta noche tienes que robarme el pan del horno.

Pronto se fue Juan y compró un vestido de padre, un libro de oración, un velís y un galón de vino. Esa noche tenía el rey munchos veladores para que

cuidaran el pan en el horno, pero cuando vieron a Juan viniendo hacia donde estaban ellos, dijieron:

—No es más que un padre que anda rezando. Déjenlo pasar.

Llegó Juan en donde estaban ellos y les preguntó qué estaban haciendo.

—Estamos velando el pan en este horno porque esta noche va a venir Juan a querérselo robar.

—O, ese Juan, ¡qué travieso es! ¿Quieren un trago de vino? —les preguntó Juan.

Ellos pronto aceptaron el vino y en tanto que el aire se bebieron todo el galón de vino y se emborracharon y se quedaron dormidos. Juan sacó el pan, lo echó en el velís y se fue para su casa.

Otro día fue a llevarle el pan al rey. El rey le dijo:

—Este robo no cuenta, pues esos veladores se emborracharon. Fue muy fácil robarme el pan. Para creer que sí eres ladrón fino, debes venir a robarme todo el dinero que yo tengo y si me lo robas entonces sí eres ladrón fino.

Esta vez se fue Juan a comprar un vestido de ángel y un cabestro. Esa noche se fue a la capilla del rey y se subió para la torre donde estaba la campana y se puso a repicarla. El rey le dijo a la reina:

—Voy a ver quién repica la campana a estas horas de la noche.

Cuando llegó a la capilla, miró para arriba y fue viendo a un ángel en la torre. Se acercó más a ver si en verdad era un ángel. Cuando se acercó le dijo Juan:

—Yo soy un ángel que ha venido por ti para llevarte al cielo. Dios quiere llevarte en cuerpo y alma para que no sufras en este mundo. ¿Quieres irte?

—¡Sí, sí! —respondió! el rey—. Soy buen cristiano y sí quiero ir al cielo.

—Bueno —dijo Juan—, pero antes de poder llevarte conmigo al cielo, tienes que poner tu dinero en un solo lugar para que lo usen los pobres.

—Lo que usted diga —respondió el rey. Y se fue muy apurado para el palacio.

Cuando volvió el rey a la capilla, le preguntó Juan:

—¿Pusites todo tu dinero en un solo lugar?

—Sí —le dijo el rey—, lo dejé en un rincón junto a la puerta. Ya estoy listo para irme con usted.

—Bueno, préndete de este cabestro y cierra los ojos.

Juan empezó a jalar el cabestro y cuando ya iba muy alto, lo soltó. Fue tan fuerte el golpe que se dio el rey cuando pegó al suelo que no supo de él. Se abajó Juan, levantó al rey en brazos y se lo llevó al gallinero. Luego se fue derecho donde había puesto el rey todo su dinero y se lo llevó para su casa.

Otro día en la madrugada cuando estaban cantando los gallos estaba volviendo el rey de su desmayo. Al mirar las gallinas el rey pensó:

—Quizás en la gloria también hay gallinas.

Más tarde fue la criada a echarles de comer a las gallinas y se encontró con el rey caído entre las gallinas. Le ayudó a levantarse y lo llevó al palacio más muerto que vivo.

Otro día vino Juan a traerle su dinero.

¡Ahora sí creo que eres ladrón fino! —dijo el rey—. Te doy la mitad de mi dinero y también te doy a mi hija para que te cases con ella.

Juan Tonto no aceptó el dinero porque él ya tenía tanto de lo suyo, pero a su hija sí quiso...ya no era tan tonto. Pronto se casaron y vivieron felices toda su vida. ✢

El León, El Tigre y el Oso Don José

En una vez había un hombre y una mujer que vivían en el monte con un hijo y una hija. Este muchacho y la muchacha estaban muy jóvenes cuando sus padres se murieron y ellos se quedaron solos en la casa.

Pronto aprendieron a vivir solos y un día la muchacha le dijo a su hermano:

—Hermano, ahora que nos quedamos solos vamos a prometer no casarnos nunca, ni tú, ni yo.

—Bueno —dijo el muchacho, y los dos se prometieron no casarse nunca.

El muchacho tenía un león, un tigre y un oso que se llamaba don José que él había criado desde que era pequeño. Estos animales eran muy listos y hacían todo lo que su amo les mandaba. Para cuidar a su hermanita, el muchacho salía a cazar venado en las montañas con la ayuda de sus amigos animales.

Un día salió el muchacho con sus animalitos a cazar. Ese día, un gigante llegó a la casa. Entró y halló a la muchacha solita. El gigante se enamoró de la muchacha y la muchacha del gigante. El gigante le preguntó que si quería casarse con él. Entonces la muchacha le dijo:

—Yo y mi hermano tenemos prometidos no casarnos.

El gigante le dijo que podía él matar al hermano si le permitía casarse con él. La muchacha le dijo:

—Bueno, pero no sé para qué rumbo sale mi hermano cuando va a cazar todos los días.

—O —dijo el gigante—, esta tarde cuando venga le preguntas para qué rumbo va a salir mañana.

La muchacha le contestó que le diría en la mañana para qué rumbo iría su hermano ese día. El gigante se fue de la casa antes de que viniera el hermano.

En la tarde cuando llegó el hermano a la casa, su hermana estaba muy contenta con él. Cuando se sentaron a comer la muchacha le dijo:

—Hermanito, ¿Para qué rumbo vas a salir mañana?

—¡Ah! —dijo el hermano—.¿Tú me quieres jugar traición?

—¿Por qué me preguntas eso? ¡No! —dijo la muchacha—. ¿Cuándo es que yo te quería jugar traición, hermano mío?

—Bueno —dijo el muchacho—. Mañana voy a salir hacia el rumbo de la mesa blanca.

El muchacho no durmió en toda la noche, pensando en qué traición le quería jugar su hermana. Otro día se fue con sus animalitos y con su rifle.

A poco rato que se fue el joven, llegó el gigante. La muchacha le dijo para dónde se había ido su hermano. De una vez se dirigió el gigante al rumbo de la mesa blanca. Cuando el pobre muchacho vido venir al gigante, malició de una vez que su hermana le había jugado una traición. El gigante empezó a pelear con el muchacho. El muchacho le daba balazos pero el gigante traía un remedio que pronto le curaba las heridas.

Luego que el muchacho se cansó de pelear con el gigante, llamó a sus animalitos y les dijo:

—Ahora es el tiempo que deben de defender a su señor amito. ¡Devoren a ese gigante!

El oso don José de una vez le quitó la botella con el remedio al gigante y la tiró sobre una piedra, y luego en un momento lo mataron. Cuando ya lo mataron les dijo su amo:

—¡Ahora sí vamos a platicar con mi hermana!

Cuando llegaron a la casa, el muchacho vido las huellas del gigante en el patio. Cuando entró le dijo a su hermana:

—Adiós, hermanita, ya me voy. Veo que tú no quieres estar conmigo. Tú eres traicionera. Ya maté al gigante, ahora quédate sola, y ¡que Dios te ayude!

La muchacha lloraba y le decía que no se fuera pero él llamó a sus animalitos y se fueron. Caminaron muncho hasta que llegaron a la casa de una viejita que vivía en las afueras de una ciudad. El muchacho tocó la puerta y le pidió posada.

—Pueden quedarse todo lo que quieran —les dijo la viejita—, pues estoy sola y me gustaría tener gente como usted y sus animalitos en casa.

—Gracias, abuelita —le dijo el joven—. ¿Podemos pagarle con la carne?

—Sí, me gustaría eso —dijo la viejita.

Entonces él mandó a sus animalitos a las montañas por un venado. Los animalitos presto volvieron con un venado.

La mujer prendió la lumbre y preparó la carne. Pronto se sentaron a comer y cuando estaban comiendo le preguntó el joven:

—¿Qué hay de nuevo en la ciudad, abuelita?

—No hay más de nuevo que aquí hay una serpiente que manda que le den una doncella para comer. Ya no queda nadien más que la princesa y mañana se la va a comer. El rey tiene prometido que él que mata la serpiente se casará con la princesa. Pero hasta ahora nadien se ha atrevido.

El muchacho miró a sus animalitos y pronto dijo:

—Yo me voy a casar con la princesa.

Otro día nomás se levantó y se fue a ver a la princesa. Cuando iba llegando vido a la princesa sentada en el balcón esperando que llegara la serpiente a comérsela. El muchacho cuando llegó dijo:

—¿Qué estás haciendo ahí tan triste?

—Ah —dijo la princesa—, estoy esperando una serpiente que viene a comerme.

Entonces el joven le dijo:

—Si te casas conmigo yo me atrevo a matar la serpiente.

La muchacha le dijo:

—Entonces, ¡ve! Yo tengo miedo de que si tú te quedas más aquí, te come a tí junto conmigo.

—No tengas miedo —le dijo el joven—. Prométeme que te casas conmigo y yo la mato.

La princesa le prometió casarse con él. Cuando llegó la serpiente el joven llamó a sus animalitos y les dijo:

—Don León, y don Tigre y don José, ¡devoren esa serpiente!

Los animalitos en tanto que el aire mataron la serpiente. Esta serpiente tenía siete cabezas.Cuando la mataron, el joven le cortó las siete lenguas y le dijo a don José que se las tragara.Luego fueron y le dijieron a la princesa que habían matado la serpiente. Ella vino a ver si era verdad, y cuando vido la serpiente muerta, le dio al joven una mascada y un anillo.

—Estos son un símbolo de mi promesa de casarme contigo —le dijo al joven.

Él los aceptó y dijo que volvía el otro día. Se fue para la casa de la viejita, y la muchacha se fue para el palacio del rey. Poco después, un moro iba pasando por donde estaba la serpiente muerta y se bajó de su burro y se le cortó a la serpiente las siete cabezas y se fue caminando. Cuando alcanzó a la princesa, le dijo a ella:

—Ya maté la serpiente. Mañana tienes que casarte conmigo.

La princesa nomás se rió pero no le dijo nada al moro. No sabía que él le había cortado las cabezas de la serpiente y que iba a decirle al rey que mató la serpiente.

Cuando vido el rey las siete cabezas de la serpiente, le dijo al moro:

—Mañana te casas con la princesa y tendremos tres días de fiesta.

Les mandó a sus sirvientes que prepararan la fiesta. Otro día se empezaron las fiestas y el joven supo. Le preguntó a la viejita:

—¿Quiere tener una fiesta?

—Con muncho gusto, nietecito —le respondió la viejita.

Entonces el joven llamó al tigre y le mandó que fuera para el palacio del rey y que le diera la mascada a la princesa. El joven echó una cartita dentro la mascada y se la dio al tigre y le dijo que no fuera a ofender a nadien en el castillo. El tigre se fue y cuando llegó a la sala toda la gente se asombró al ver que el animal se fue derecho adonde estaba sentada la princesa.

La princesa le quitó la mascada, sacó la carta y la leyó. Luego fue y llenó la mascada de comida y se la dio al tigre. El rey gritó:

—¡Doy cinco pesos a él que me diga adónde llega este animal!

Todos los muchachos se fueron siguiendo al tigre pero cuando iba llegando a la casa de la viejita, se volteó e hizo como que iba a atacarlos, pues se fueron ellos corriendo derecho a la fiesta.

Otro día, el segundo día de la fiesta, el joven mandó a don León la misma cosa que le había dicho al tigre. Pues, hizo lo mismo que el tigre, le entregó la mascada a la princesa, ella la llenó de comida y se la entregó al león para que la devolviera al muchacho. Cuando el león iba a salir, el rey otra vez le ofreció cinco pesos a él que le dijiera adónde llegaba el animal. Lo mismo pasó que había pasado con el tigre. Se volteó e hizo como que iba a atacarlos, pues se fueron ellos corriendo derecho a la fiesta. Le dijieron al rey que no podían seguir al león, de modo que no supieron adónde había llegado el león.

Otro día iba a ser la última fiesta y el joven llamó a don José el oso y le dijo:

—'Hora va usted a la fiesta, don José, y no se vaya a emborrachar, ¿oyó?

Don José meneaba la cabeza que sí. Cuando llegó don José a la fiesta, toda la gente se hizo para un lado del salón. Don José se fue para donde estaba sentada la princesa y le entregó la mascada. Entonces la princesa llevó a don José para el banquete acompañada por el rey y la reina y el moro.

Cuando estaban a la mesa del banquete, el rey empezó a darle vino a don José hasta que se emborrachó. Luego le dio un barril lleno de vino y la mascada con comida. Otra vez el rey mandó a los muchachos que fueran adónde llegaba el animal. Como don José andaba borracho, iba cayéndose y los muchachos lo siguieron hasta la casa de la viejita. Luego se fueron a decirle al rey adónde había llegado don José. Entonces el rey dijo que otro día iban a tener otra fiesta más y que los muchachos fueran a invitar al dueño de los animalitos. Pronto fueron los muchachos e invitaron al joven y a la viejita.

Otro día cuando llegó el muchacho al castillo del rey, le dijo al rey que él quería platicar con él a solas. Entonces el muchacho y el rey entraron a un cuarto y se pusieron a platicar. El joven le dijo al rey:

—Su majestad, ¿ha visto usted campanas sin badajos?

—No —dijo el rey—. ¿Por qué me preguntas eso?

—O, dijo el joven—, nomás porque quiero saber si ha visto campanas sin badajos. ¿Y ha visto usted cabezas sin lenguas?

—No —respondió el rey.

Luego el joven le dijo al rey:

—Tráigame usted las cabezas de la serpiente a ver si tienen lenguas.

El joven llamó a don José y le dijo que le entregara las lenguas de las cabezas de la serpiente. Cuando el rey vido las cabezas sin lenguas y las lenguas que trujo el oso, llamó al moro y le dijo que no podía casarse con su hija porque no había matado la serpiente. Lo mandó a trabajar y luego le dijo al dueño de los animalitos que como fue él que mató la serpiente, podía casarse con la princesa y que tendrían tres días de fiestas.

El moro se fue llorando a su trabajo y decía:

—¡La serpiente no tiene lenguas, la serpiente no tiene lenguas!

Siguieron los tres días de fiestas. Mientras tanto, la hermana del joven había estudiado libros mágicos y en el día que iban a casarse el joven y la princesa, la hermana se apareció de repente en el palacio. Estaba celosa y amargada estando sola y había venido a matar a su hermano. Cuando llegó se comportó muy mielosa y le dijo al rey que quería ver a su hermano solo en un cuarto. Cuando él entró al cuarto con ella, la hermana empezó a alisarlo, hablándole dulcemente. De repente, sacó los dientes del gigante que llevaba con ella y se los enterró en su hermano.

Tan pronto que como le enterró los dientes, cayó el joven muerto. La hermana se desapareció y se fue para el monte. Luego que el rey vido que no salía el joven, entró al cuarto y lo vido muerto. No supo de qué se había muerto y todos junto con la princesa lloraban muncho.

Otro día le hicieron un gran funeral y lo enterraron. El rey temía que los animalitos se volverían locos ahora que no estaba el muchacho para controlarlos, entonces le dijo a sus sirvientes que los encerrara en un cuarto en el castillo. Los pobres animalitos se quedaron solitos y no vieron a su amo muerto. A los tres días el rey abrió la puerta y de una vez empezaron a buscar a su amo. Ellos siguieron las huellas de la gente hasta el camposanto. Cuando llegaron al sepulcro se pusieron a escarbar hasta que sacaron a su amito. Se pusieron a llorar amargamente.

Don José se puso a alisar el cuerpo del muchacho y notó algo extraño. Al tocarlo con cuidado, sintió los dientes del gigante. Los sacó y de una vez ¡se levantó el joven vivo! Pronto se fue con sus animalitos para el castillo del rey. Todos se quedaron asombrados cuando lo vieron, pero él les dijo que no tuvieran miedo, que su hermana lo había encantado con los dientes del gigante. Él les platicó toda la historia de él y su hermana y cómo ella lo había traicionado esa vez con el gigante. Desde entonces no volvió a ver a su hermana. Él y la princesa y sus animalitos vivieron muy a gusto por munchos años. Pueda que todavía estén vivos. ✛

Juan Burumbete

Cuanto hay vivía un hombre que se llamaba Juan Burumbete. Este Juan era tan flojo que no tenía alientos ni para lavarse, de modo que siempre andaba hecho roña. Un día de verano estaba Juan sentado en la resolana con la cara y las manos llenas de moscas, como a las moscas les gusta la roña. Le estaban molestando a Juan y él estaba pegándoles cada rato, pero no muy apriesa porque no quería cansarse. Empezó a enfadarse con las moscas y hacer más fuerza de correrlas. Él estaba sentado contando las moscas que mataba. Se dio una manotada en la cara y mató siete moscas de una vez. Y luego se pegó en el brazo y mató un montón.

—¡O! —dijo Juan—, yo soy muy valiente, de un moquete mato siete, y de un rempujón, un montón.

Estaba diciendo la misma cosa Juan cada rato porque había matado tantas moscas. Estaba tan contento que fue para la casa del herrero y le dijo que le hiciera un letrero para su sombrero que dijiera:

"Este es Juan Burumbete
Que de un moquete mata a siete
Y de un rempujón
Un montón"

Juan fue y se sentó junto al camino real donde se sentaba siempre a cuidar a la gente pasar, sintiéndose muy orgulloso. Cuando la gente se encontraba con él en el camino real y leían el letrero, abrían los ojos muy grandes y salían huyendo. Ellos pensaban que el letrero quería decir que había matado a munchos hombres, no moscas, y ellos tenían miedo de que los fuera a matar a ellos también.

Alguna de la gente que vido a Juan fue a decirle al rey que estaba un hombre muy valiente y muy peligroso en su reino, uno que sabe munchos modos de matar. Cuando el rey oyó esto, estaba sorprendido y dijo:

—¡Dios ha escuchado mis oraciones! Los moros mataron a mi hijo Macario y si este hombre es tan valiente como era mi hijo, él podrá vengar la muerte de mi hijo.

Mandó a llamar a Juan, que todavía estaba sentado cerca del camino real matando moscas. Él era tan flojo que no se había movido de ahí. Todavía estaba sentado en el sol como siempre y se espantó cuando oyó que el rey lo había llamado. Él se fue siguiendo al sirviente del rey todo el camino hasta el palacio.

—¿Eres tan valiente como dice el letrero? —preguntó el rey.

—Sí, su majestad, de un moquete mato siete, y de un rempujón, un montón —respondió Juan Burumbete.

—Bueno —le dijo el rey—, quiero que te alistes para pelear contra los moros tan pronto como puedas, y si sales victorioso, te doy a mi hija, la princesa, para que te cases con ella.

Juan tenía miedo de decirle al rey que nomás moscas había matado. Entonces, dijo:

—Sí, su majestad —y se fue para la casa.

Otro día volvió Juan para el castillo del rey. Entonces el rey le dio el caballo que era del Macario. Este caballo era muy grande y soberbio y trotaba con su cabeza levantada al aire.

—Ves —le dijo el rey—, el caballo de Macario está listo para vengarse de la muerte de su amo. Él te llevará muy ligero a la batalla.

Juan vido el gigante animal y tembló de miedo. Él nunca había montado a caballo de ninguna clase, menos un caballo de guerra tan animoso para pelear. No sabía cómo hacer para que no vieran los otros soldados su ignorancia. Pensó un rato y luego les dijo:

—Bueno, compañeros, amárrenme en el caballo.

Sus compañeros se asustaron y decían uno al otro:

—¡Qué tiene ese hombre? ¿Pero cómo va a pelear este hombre amarrado?

Pero hicieron lo que les mandaba y se fue prendiéndose de la silla con las dos manos. Los soldados meneaban la cabeza y no pudieron creer lo que estaban mirando. Pero vieron el letrero en su sombrero y pensaban que fácil tendría una treta para jugarles a los moros. Y pronto salieron en sus caballos cruzando el llano haciendo muncho polvo.

Caminaron por largo tiempo y ya iba Juan con las nalgas bien adoloridas. Quería bajarse del caballo pero sabía que no podía porque iba amarrado en la silla. Cuando se acercaron al campo de batalla, iba muy cansado. Él empezó a apenarse y pensó:

—¿Cómo voy hacer yo para que no sepan mis compañeros que soy un cobarde y que no sé andar a caballo, cuanto menos pelear a caballo?

Cuando ya llegaron al campo de batalla, ya sabía qué hacer. Paró a los otros soldados y les dijo:

—No quiero que vayan conmigo. Espérenme aquí. Yo iré solo.

Los soldados estaban espantados pero dejaron a Juan que fuera solo a pelear. Se fue solo hasta que llegó a un cañón muy hondo cerca del lugar en donde estaban los moros esperando el encuentro. Cuando el caballo de Marcario oyó el pito de guerra,

empezó a levantarse de pies, porque era un caballo de guerra con experiencia y había peleado contra los moros munchas veces.

A Juan Burumbete le dio muncho miedo, y empezó a llorar en voz alta, y decía:

—¡Ay, Dios, me mata este caballo!

Los moros pensaron que decía:

—¡Ay, Dios, ya revivió Macario!

Reconocieron al caballo de Macario y estaban tan asustados pensando que Macario había resucitado que salieron huyendo todos para el rumbo del cañón. No cuidaban adónde iban y se fueron todos en el cañón y se mataron. Cuando Juan vido lo que había acontecido, fue y les dijo a sus compañeros que lo estaban esperando:

—Pues, ya maté a todos los moros.

Ellos no podían creerlo. Dijieron:

—¿Cómo hicites eso tan pronto? —y se fueron para el campo de la batalla. Fueron al cañón y se encontraron con todos los moros muertos al fondo del cañón. De una vez mandaron a un mensajero a darle noticia al rey de la victoria del Juan.

El rey estaba tan contento que los moros habían perdido la guerra.

—Al fin, la muerte de Macario ha sido vengado. En paz descanse —dijo el rey.

Luego llamó a su hija y le dijo:

—Yo le prometí a Juan Burumbete que podía casarse contigo si ganaba la batalla, y lo ha hecho.

La princesa se soltó llorando.

—¡Yo no me caso con ese hombre tan roñoso! —dijo ella.

—No te apenes, mi hija —dijo el rey—. Ese mal tiene remedio.

El rey le dio a Juan jabón de lejía para que tomara un buen baño. Y le dio un vestido muy lujoso para que se lo pusiera. Cuando Juan salió del baño, ya no parecía aquel Juan Burumbete roñoso de más antes. Y también ya no era flojo. Cuando lo vido la princesa tan galán, no refunfuñó más. Se casaron y vivieron felices por toda la vida. ✣

Epilogue

GRANDMA WELCOMES ME INTO HER *sala*, where she sits with a pen and scrap of paper in her hand. "I want to write a letter, but I don't know what to write," she says as I sit beside her. A scrawl of random words covers the paper from edge to edge, each phrase beginning with "Dear . . ." I lean over to hug her and she presses her face into my chest. "I'm so glad you came," she says, "I've been waiting all day. It seems so empty when you're not here."

We sit quietly for a long time, looking around the still room. Paintings on the wall made by her late son Robert show the Chimayó landscape of years gone by: the *tazoleras* that belonged to Don Nicolás next door, with their rusted roofs and weathered log walls; the Santuario with two giant cottonwood trees arched over it's front gate, framing the church with storybook grace; and a sagging wooden gate and a driveway to an adobe house half hidden by cottonwood limbs. The paintings hang crookedly as they have for decades, flanked by photos of Grandma and Grandpa Abedón on their wedding day, looking young and a bit frightened, and of my mother and her brothers as smiling little children.

Grandma and Abedón bought the couch beneath the paintings from Bloch's furniture store in Española in the early 1930s, along with the accompanying easy chair. For the beautiful Persian carpet on the floor, she and Abedón traded some blankets he had woven. The back of the couch is adorned with one of those same classic old Chimayó blankets, finely woven with intricate designs as only Abedón could produce. Another of his weavings, this one in a Rio Grande striped pattern and made of wool that grandma carded and dyed, covers the seat of the couch.

My eyes wander to the opposite side of the room and to the first television in the house. Bought in the early 1950s, it hasn't functioned for as long as I can remember, but I can imagine its small, round screen flickering with the old shows that I would watch on summer evenings as a child. The record player in the other corner also remains in its familiar place, long outdated records neatly stacked below. Grandma doesn't watch TV or listen to music. She never did. Instead, she passes her days worrying the beads of a rosary with her wrinkled hands or staring out the window toward the house across the road where she was born more than a century ago.

This sanctuary-like room evokes the past with the force of emotion that runs deep. Almost no other piece of the Chimayó world I knew as a child remains intact. As Grandma so often bemoans, *todo ha cambiado*, everything has changed.

The wonderful contents of the old *dispensa* that I marveled at as a child were hauled to the dump or to storage when my wife and I remodeled the building and made it into a home. I sit at a word processor writing these lines in the very spot where Grandpa Reyes's looms once stood. I drove by the *arbolitos* the other day, rushing down the paved highway on some errand, and saw workmen hauling away the last of the dead fruit trees that Grandma and I used to visit. Even the Ortega acequia has changed. Where it used to flow free through the Enchanted Garden, it is now confined to a buried plastic pipe, and the cottonwoods that overarched its banks are shriveling and dying.

This cool, darkened *sala* remains, though, a change-proof shelter that survived the blast that swept remnants of old days from most of Chimayó. Yet even this house, like the other old buildings and Grandma herself, is slowly teetering toward collapse.

The cuentos occupy this room with us, in manuscript form on my lap and, more vividly, in our memories. Grandma knows I'm nearing the end of my work on these cuentos, and she grabs my hand and implores me, in Spanish, for Spanish is all she speaks to me now: "I wrote those stories that you have, I put them down on paper myself. They are my stories. Give them back to me when you're done, *tengas*? I want to keep them with me."

I give Grandma a copy of my manuscript, which makes her smile, but as I place the written cuentos in her hands I realize that these aren't hers any more than they are my mother's or mine. Grandma did write them down by hand some twenty-five or thirty years ago, and her records formed the basis for my mother's laborious transcriptions and translations, which, in turn, gave me a starting point for my own reworking. Nevertheless, the cuentos don't belong to any individual in the long line of people that transmitted them generation to generation. They belong to this place and its idiosyncratic human community, which embraces many people and many years.

What does belong to Grandma is her story, and it's one that remains to be fully told. The cuentos, together with my memories of her telling them, bring one small piece to light, but there is much more. Glimpses are revealed in the cards, letters, and endless notebooks that she kept. One notebook still lies by her bed, although the entries end after several pages on which she repeated over and over the news that her youngest son had died, as if the repetition might help her accept the cold hard fact of his passing.

And now she can no longer put words to paper at all.

Grandma holds me close, and my five-year-old daughter comes into the room and looks at Grandma with awe. When Jennifer asks me why Grandma is sad, how can I tell her of the lifetime of joy and sadness that has distilled to the deep melancholy that commands Grandma's moods? I just tell her to give Grandma a hug, and she does, and Grandma's face glows and comes to life. "This little girl will bring a lot of joy into your lives," she says, and the ninety-seven years separating them evaporate in an embrace of mutual affection.

Amid the despair that I sometimes feel at seeing places change and old ones pass on, I find comfort in this embrace of *viejita* and child, past and the future. Life goes on, and I'm nudged a bit closer to learning life's most persistent and hard-to-learn lesson, the one about letting go. It's a lesson that Grandma knows so well, and it's made a bit easier knowing that these cuentos, along with their cargo of wisdom, humor, and love, have survived another century of tumult and will pass into a new millennium. Will they persist merely as historical artifacts or will they inform and entertain new generations in the fast-paced world that Grandma is leaving behind?

I'll tell Jennifer the story of the *Caballero de la Pluma* tonight and see.